HERE TO STAY
Americans with Intellectual and Developmental Disabilities

MICHAEL T. BAILEY

America Star Books
Frederick, Maryland

© 2016 by Michael T. Bailey.

All rights reserved. No part of this book may be reproduced, stored in a retrieval system or transmitted in any form or by any means without the prior written permission of the publishers, except by a reviewer who may quote brief passages in a review to be printed in a newspaper, magazine or journal.

First printing

America Star Books has allowed this work to remain exactly as the author intended, verbatim, without editorial input.

Softcover 9781680903904
PUBLISHED BY AMERICA STAR BOOKS, LLLP
www.americastarbooks.pub
Frederick, Maryland

"Let us unite in a revolution
To eliminate primitive stereotypes, and
To establish a culture that focuses
The full force of science and democracy
On the systematic empowerment of every
Person to live to his or her god
Given potential.

No soldier has ever died in a better cause!"

Justin Dart, Jr.
Statement of Conscience
1998

"To accept one's past—one's history—is not the same
As drowning in it.
An invented past can never be used:
It cracks and crumbles under the pressure
Of life like clay in a season of drought."

James Baldwin

INTRODUCTION

Why is it so difficult for Americans with disabilities, particularly those with intellectual and developmental disabilities (IDD), to gain acceptance in mainstream society? The answer is as old as the republic itself. The suffering of people with disabilities is mostly overlooked and ignored. That reality is interwoven in every moment of United States history. We were never 'not there.' Nor were we ever welcome. As with all injustice it is time to break the silence.

Americans with IDD are not now and never have been taken seriously. The disability industrial complex, that giant money making, career promoting monolith that dominates their lives, is only too anxious to speak for them. There are non-disabled interests and there are disabled interests. They are not the same. Authentic voices come only from persons with disabilities. And their voices are virtually absent from official history books. More common are the voices of experts and bureaucrats and do-gooders who, upon retirement, look back on their careers and say 'disability has been good to me.'

Far from the egalitarian principles claimed in United States History classes the country was founded on principles of exclusion and elitism. The truth is that every category of person not a white male property owner has, from the beginning, had to fight desperately for a piece of the American pie. To put our faith in the notion that the mere passage of time will mean acceptance is to do so at our peril. Like other groups who fought and sacrificed people with IDD will take their freedom. Nothing happens by accident.

Change is the result of hard work.

I have organized this book into two parts. Part I is a history of the United States with emphasis on the exclusion of groups not part of the founders' vision. The parallels between racism and the disregard for the humanity of people with disabilities are obvious. I have not written this book for professional historians or academics (much as I love them.) Rather I have tried to tell this story from the perspective of a person with IDD who is discovering their history for the first time and asking 'where do I fit in?'

I had originally planned to include several dozen stories written by people with IDD. They were to be presented without comment, background or explanation. Some legal issues arose regarding the sufficiency of releases. Since this book involves a commercial transaction it was agreed that from an abundance of caution I would not include them. See Postscript for information on how to obtain them in a non-commercial way. Since learning to listen and respect people is a key to progress I have decided to leave in my comments about where those stories came from and the process I used to obtain them.

For some years, under a contract with the Developmental Disabilities Council of Oregon, I edited and published *The People First Connection*. (PFC). During those years I provided supports to dozens of people with IDD who wished to write. Through a series of workshops or one on one appointments the writer and I worked on getting their words down on paper.

No one was a confident writer. Some of the articles are the work of people who actually cannot write. For me, this was a 'learn as you go' experience. My commitment was to make sure that what was on paper was authentic. No two of the writers were the same. Some had vast amounts of enthusiasm and a bottomless well of thoughts, experiences and ideas they wanted to share. Others had a very hard time just imagining what there was about their life that was something to write about.

I learned that there were no short cuts. To do these required two things; privacy and time. And a third, respect. I undertook this project with a deep respect for the individuals I intended to find.

Respect requires humility. To make contact with others abelist attitudes, privilege, a sense of entitlement and superiority have to go. This is true of all human contact. It is perhaps more true with folks with intellectual disabilities. Everyone represented here and pretty much all others I know have a shared memory of being put down, patronized or just ignored. That memory is always with them. There are plenty of good reasons not to trust someone from outside their community.

Part II is reflection on the specific history of Americans with disabilities. Why were they invisible? When not invisible who told their story? A lot of damage was done by people with good intentions. No group has the right to speak for another. What has been missing all these years are people with disabilities speaking for themselves. All else is bogus. Why institutions? Why eugenics? Why poverty? Why isolation? Why infantilism? Why unemployment? That people with IDD are finally seizing their own lives is a testament to the human spirit and its indomitable ability to survive and persevere. Today the future may or may not be bright. But it is brighter than it has ever been. How did we get here?

In my years as a lawyer for the American Indian Movement one thing I learned is that no one needed any advice from me about how to be an Indian. I came into that community to learn and not to teach.

When I began to have lots of personal interaction with folks with IDD that lesson played an important role. No one with a disability needed me to teach them anything about their reality. I have always thought of myself as their student. In turn my friends with IDD have been the most generous of teachers.

In the process of compiling these stories my determination to provide time, privacy and respect was repaid over and over. Earning trust was the crucial factor in achieving my goal of making certain these stories are real and not filtered. Some of them are raw. How could they not be? Each of these writers took this seriously and worked closely with me to get their story told right. Both of us were happy and pleased when that last proofreading was over and we could agree "that's me. That is good."

We would start with ideas for possible topics. Sometimes that was easy and other times it seemed impossible. These writings are going to be presented with no explanation or interpretation. It is left to the reader to draw any conclusions. My only comment is that people living lives of relative community integration had a lot more to say then those who did not. The stories are pretty obvious as to which is which.

Sometimes these face to face sessions would last an hour. Sometimes many hours and in some cases happened over a period of days. Ideally the writer would write. When that was impossible it was more a matter or me taking dictation. I was very careful not to substitute my words for theirs. Sometimes it was painful to watch someone grapple so hard trying to express what they meant. But that too was a part of the process.

Before these sessions began we agreed that whatever was put down on paper would be edited by me for spelling and grammar. Partly that was to make them more easily read. But it was also to avoid embarrassment by demonstrating something the writers did not want people to know. To get these done required mutual trust and respect. And in that I think we succeeded.

Lastly each of these articles was carefully read back to the author. By then any spelling or grammar edits I made were completed. For me this was the most important step. I needed each of them to listen carefully, ask any questions they had and affirmatively tell me that, indeed, this was their work.

Since the PFC lost funding and ceased publication these stories have been on my computer and from time to time I have realized that taken alone they are just a story. But taken together they are a valuable collection of life as an American with an IDD. Thus the inspiration for this book. These stories are both too important and too rare to gather dust.

When the stories first began to appear in the *PFC* reaction varied. Most important was that the writers were delighted and helped the project along by encouraging their friends to participate. Self-advocates, that is others with IDD were very supportive. Not only in Oregon but around the country.

At the same time it opened a chasm that I have come to expect. Two strains of ugly that run too frequently through the professional community and hovers around people with IDD. The first of those is the habit of underestimating people. The other is a sort of proprietary sense of 'my self-advocates.'

The proprietary part came from providers who were uncomfortable with 'their people' having unfettered freedom to state their opinions. Often those opinions were different than they might have been had their provider/supervisor been present. The other group were those with a history of being 'advisors' to People First groups. There was a sense of suspicion that someone else was messing with 'their' people. At the time I found it surprising and then annoying. Since I have learned to expect it. People's livelihoods are very easily threatened.

More significant was the underestimating of the sophistication of the writers. "How could they have possibly written those things? I don't believe it" was a rather common reaction. The most memorable example is described in the next paragraph. That comment has stayed with me over the years and has provided more determination than I may otherwise have had to assure authenticity in the writings.

I edited another publication at the same time. There had just been a major class action law suit settlement in Oregon. The result was a revolutionary change in the way state services are provided. Everyone eligible has a right to services here. There are no wait lists. The case settlement is the foundation upon which Oregon's current system of self-directed brokerage based services is built.

Among the first person to benefit from that settlement was the adult son of one of the named plaintiffs. Within a short time he had his own apartment many miles away from his parents and a support system to make it work. I went to his apartment to interview him. Both of his parents were present but did not participate in our interview.

I wrote the story up and quoted this young man quite a lot. I sent the draft off to my editor. In a very short time the phone rang. The editor was incensed and said 'did you actually go see him? Did you make this up? **Everybody knows he can't talk!?"** (Emphasis supplied).

I referred him to the parents as witnesses. They confirmed our interview. The story was published as written.

"Everybody knows he can't talk" has stuck with me and at the time provoked a series of unflattering images. A very teachable moment for me. The images were ones of disability conferences which this young man attended along with his family. I could plainly see him in a corner, rather shyly being inconspicuous but enjoying the moment nevertheless. Around him swirled various officials, officers, functionaries, etc., all colleagues of his mother, and all saying a cursory 'hello' to him and nothing else. Everyone knew he could not talk because no one had ever taken him seriously as a human being and attempted a conversation in his comfort zone. He talks just fine. All you need is a little respect and some desire to hear what he has to say.

To me that interaction has taken on a lot more than just an anecdote. Underestimating the insights of people with IDD is endemic throughout the service system. Non-disabled interests talk exclusively to other non-disabled interests. Often about how devoted they are to 'those people.' People they really don't know. Or care to know. Good intentions are not enough. Indeed, as we shall see, good intentions have mostly been at the root of the gigantic state sponsored crimes against people with IDD. They continue to be.

Eugenics, infantilism, institutions, exploitation and exclusion have all marked people with IDD.

I wondered why. Is it disability that excludes people? Or is it a far larger issue endemic to the United States? Is it true that inclusion is a national trait? Or is it exclusion? Do homilies like the Pledge of Allegiance and the Gettysburg Address accurately portray the USA? Or are they hoaxes?

How many people are we talking about? Of course each individual life is different. But for sheer numbers people with intellectual and developmental disabilities are a big chunk.

According to the web site of the Arc of the US an estimated 4.6 million Americans have the label. The Arc's site however is based on a study done in the 1990s and is forthcoming in its clarity in emphasizing that number as an estimate. The Center for Disease Control has different numbers. It makes no difference. The fact is that the numbers of people both living and dead are huge. What happened to them all?

In 2012 the Bethesda Center estimated the number at somewhere between 4.6 and 7.7 million. That wide disparity is based on what percentage of the population one regards as having the label. Is it 1.25% or 2.5%. The Center for Disease control claims the number to be as high as 15%.

According to the Bethesda Center there is one number we can agree on. There are today at least 34,000 Americans with intellectual and developmental disabilities locked up in state run institutions. How many are in privately run institutions is unknown.

Why have all of these people left so little first person record of their lives? The short answer is that no one cared.

Another number we can count on is two. That is the number of states in the United States that do not have an institution. Only Oregon and Alabama are 100% committed to community based living. All others rely, to a greater or lesser degree, on institutional placement in some conglomerate facility. Generally in a pastoral setting, far away from family, community or the modern world. On the edge of too many small towns are huge buildings with elaborate grounds bearing uplifting names like "Sunshine Acres," "Fairview", "Shangri-La", "River Place", etc. All masquerade as lovely 'homes' when in fact they are more like prisons and increasingly operate more as a public works project to provide economic well-being to the non-disabled interests they actually represent. Every one of them is a disgrace.

While enjoying these snippets of lives of Americans with disabilities I hope the reader will also ponder how he or she can expose the false notes in those arias with which our official shepherds lull their flocks. Let us go beyond platitudes. Survival depends on it.

A note on the title. In Lakota culture a warrior would sometimes leap from his pony and drive his lance deep into the prairie soil. He would then calmly tie his ankle to the lance with a rawhide lace. Thus 'staked out' he would turn and face his enemy. His message was clear. I have run as far as I intend to run. Now it is you or me. I am 'here to stay.'

Eternal gratitude to my friends in the disability rights movement who were and are so generous in mentoring me. I think especially of people who have left us. My hope is that some of their brilliance and courage will live in the pages of this book. Paul Longmore, Laura Hershey, Marta Russell, Lucy Gwin, Harriett McBryde Johnson and Justin Dart, Jr., among others, never denied me a moment of their time and to them I owe a huge thanks.

Portland, Oregon
2015

PART ONE

Invisible

"Oh, no, it wasn't like this when I lived here," our commentator said. "Then there were no partitions of any kind. All of us girls slept on cots next to one another. There was never any privacy." She remembered how as a child she was frightened of "the big heads," the ones with hydrocephalus who leaned on the wall and groaned.'
"Farewell Fairview"
Michael T. Bailey

<u>NEITHER REASON NOR EXPERIENCE</u>

"The contempt we have been taught to entertain for the blacks, makes us fancy many things that are founded neither in reason nor experience; and an unwillingness to part with property so valuable a kind will furnish a thousand arguments to show the impracticability or pernicious tendency of a scheme which requires such a sacrifice…"

Alexander, Hamilton (Writings)
Letter to John Jay, March 4, 1779
The Library of America, 2001. Pg. 56.

I believe that disability is a natural and normal part of the human condition. I believe that pervasive prejudice toward those with intellectual disabilities leads to marginalizing the humanity of millions. I believe that prejudice leads to social isolation, poverty and death. I believe that these facts are so accepted as to become invisible. Tyranny cloaked in a shroud of normalcy. I believe that this dehumanizing blindness is a fundamental tenet of the American Experience.

Hamilton's quote applies equally to Americans with intellectual disabilities. To marginalize so many requires a fantasy based on neither experience nor reason. Vast profits are reaped. Of course he was not writing about disability. He was writing about the place of Afro-Americans in the newly created United States. Yet the experience of these two frequently over lapping groups is so inner twined as to require comparison.

How does one rationalize the values of a new country founded on the stated principle "all men are created equal" when the systematic exclusion of so many is the real hallmark of American history? This is what I want to talk about.

"Why is this so hard?" I have been asking that question for a long time. Institutional bias in Medicaid is a good example. People want home care. People want to age in place. People need Medicaid funding to support home care. And, as has been so richly demonstrated, it is cheaper than nursing home or institutional care. It makes sense and is sound policy. Why then has it not been adopted?

The same can be asked about compliance with special education laws, vocational rehabilitation, health care and a long list of quite easy to understand changes. Who does the system represent? Whose interests are served? Why social isolation?

Of course any change pits one group against another. Political balance and power play a roll. Power means money and that is one thing the disability rights movement lacks. But a lot of that has been made up by superior messaging and organizing. Still... No victory.

I believe there is far more to this than just traditional political posturing. I have come to believe that exclusion is such an ingrained part of the American psyche that it, like the air we breathe, is just too familiar to notice.

It is not my purpose to write an American history book. At the same time we cannot evaluate and move forward with an agenda of inclusive practice without clearly appreciating how hard social change is in the USA. I believe that when Abraham Lincoln said at Gettysburg, "One nation, conceived in liberty and dedicated to the proposition that all men are created equal" he could not have said anything more untrue.

The USA is the product of a narrow and exclusive vision. Every small addition to the number of people who truly belong has been notable for vast struggle and sacrifice. And each time the opposition has come from that core question—who belongs? Who is worthy?

It has taken many years for me to come to this conclusion and it is hard to put a finger on just when

I started to wonder less about our tactics and strategy and more about the nature of the beast itself. Do we adequately appreciate what we are up against? What I see is a rather naïve faith that things will get better based on some notion of inevitable progress. Waiting for them to 'see the light.' The history of the United States has shown us that will be a long wait.

There is an important difference between a strategy and a tactic. Good tactics attached to a flawed strategy will never produce victory. The disability rights movement has a long list of tactical successes.

All that work has paid off in progress with self-directed support, some independent living, health care access, even a bit of affordable housing. But after all this time nothing can be taken for granted. It is all precarious. True of the Americans with Disabilities Act, Social Security and support for independent living. No one can really feel secure. All of our progress is subject to sudden and devastating reversals. Why are we still struggling for the same things? Why is this so hard?

Strategy is a plan for achieving a goal. A tactic is a method for achieving that goal.

Strategy is closing institutions. Tactics are how to do it.

As part of the strategy for closure the community calls for 1,000 letters to be written to key Senators. The letters are written and delivered. Nothing happens. Something more is required. Add to the strategic plan an additional tactic of face to face visits. These are painstakingly organized and implemented. Lots of people with disabilities sit down with policy makers and tell their stories. Again nothing happens. Now what?

White papers get produced. They demonstrate that closure is cheaper. That people are happier in the community. Those papers are circulated, highlighted, etc. and nothing happens. Again, now what?

Strategy changes again to reflect the fact that what we viewed as a simple disability issue is far broader. It has local political ramifications. Small towns depend on institutions as an economic dynamo. Is job creation the reason we have institutions? Here unions can enter the picture. We try to build bridges with that union or another union. We are reduced to arguing that institutions mean more than a public works project. Nothing happens.

Any experienced advocate can add to this list of possibility. Nearly every time we execute our tactics flawlessly and yet fail. Or sometimes we succeed but with such a watered down version as to be much the same as failure.

I am not implying disrespect for our progress. People worked hard and achieved much. But it seems like every small breath of freedom requires its' own federal law to protect it. Would it not be better to simply welcome and appreciate everyone? Dr. King's famous speech expresses his dream that his own children will grow up and be judged not by the color of their skin but by the content of their character.

That same dream applies to Americans with intellectual and developmental disabilities. No group is more ignored and isolated. No group has suffered more from the dehumanizing effects of stigma. Like racism the false philosophy of ableism strikes without mercy, warning or rational basis. It just judges and separates. It hands out life sentences that exclude family, community, education, independence, employment, credit and marriage but guarantee isolation, loneliness and never ever belonging, in any real sense, to that community we call the United States of America.

At what point do we stop and reflect on the strategy? Good intentions are not strategy.

Bigger forces are at work than what we acknowledge. Exclusion is a far stronger American value than inclusion. That is hard to swallow since we are told the opposite. From the first day the United States has said one thing and done another. A nation created for white, property owning males has clung to that cadre of worthies. The rest of us fall outside of it. And that ethos is as alive and well now as it has ever been. There are parallels between the disability rights movement and those of indentured servants, small merchants, slaves, Native Americans, women, sexual minorities, field hands and immigrants that are far more obvious than we sometimes appreciate. We will not prevail alone. We have lessons to learn and alliances to forge. A successful strategy will be one with a very broad inclusive base and that includes more than just disability concerns.

There must be a strategic coalition strong enough to take on the most American habit, the preaching of one thing and the practice of another. Far from 'this land was made for you and me'. This land was made for a small elite. While that core has increased some it has never done so without taking the view that "this is mine. If you want some earn it." By that they mean take it if you can. It has always been that way.

Pondering why full enjoyment of citizenship is denied to so many Americans with intellectual and developmental disabilities it is helpful to briefly visit the origins of this nation. Founding fathers and founding documents enjoy a nearly saint cult reverence in the USA. What light can they shed on our questions about systematic discrimination and isolation? Who made those decisions? Whose interests were served? What compromises were necessary? What were the issues that could not be reconciled? Why is race the one issue about which no agreement could be reached?

The answer to that question is the same as the answer to mine: who belongs? What people are included? How did they get that way? Who is excluded? Why? Most important, is there a way for the excluded to become included? A way that works in reality and is not just a slogan on a statue. To get right down to it how do we expect a political system and culture to embrace their fellow Americans with disabilities when that system has proven incapable of successfully dealing with race?

Here is a short review of the history of the United States with an eye on getting closer to answering our central question: who belongs? Was this land really made for 'you and me'? Or was it made for 'us and them'? That is a big difference and one that plays a part in the dismissiveness that so easily makes so many Americans invisible.

IN THE BEGINNING

A short time ago the PEAK Parent Training Center of Colorado Springs, Colorado invited me to speak at one of their regional trainings. It was a simple request. They asked me to look at two United States Supreme Court cases, *Brown v. Board of Education* and *L C v Olmstead*, (much will be said later about both). I was to analyze the cases, draw comparisons between them and then address the issue of what lessons can the disability rights movement learn from the civil rights movement of the 1960s? When I accepted (happily) their invitation I had no idea how deeply I would ponder those issues.

The Brown v. Board of Education of Topeka, Kansas National Historic Site literally enshrines the original school building. With its portraits, documents, relics and presentation it is the perfect place to imagine the racially segregated south of the 1950s and the grit the parents who sued showed. As with all monumental events human brings made it happen. Not civil rights heroes or celebrities. Just a bunch of moms and dads who said 'enough' to segregation. "It stops with my child."

In 1950 schools in all of the old south were rigidly segregated by race. Everywhere were "white schools" and "colored schools." Not only in school but in all possible aspects of life the races were forcibly kept separate. It was a crime to marry someone of a different race. It was the Jim Crow South. And it was determined to stay that way.

In 1896 in the case of *Plessy v. Ferguson* the Supreme Court had ruled that as long as the separate facilities for the separate races were equal, segregation did not violate the due process clause of the fourteenth amendment. ("No state shall...deny to any person...the equal protection of the laws.)

Segregation by race was the statute, custom and Supreme Court approved law of the land. But for the parents of Topeka it would have never changed on its own. Race, as we shall see, is an issue (much like disability) that the political system of the United States cannot successfully deal with.

Against the (imagined) odds the Topeka parents argued that the education system, pretending to be equal, was in fact perpetuating inferior buildings, staff, resources and accommodations for Afro-American students. The Topeka parents were not the only plaintiffs. There were five other identical cases. All were consolidated in the Supreme Court but the opinion is commonly just "Brown."

Seventeen states filed briefs on the side of segregation. The lead counsel for integration was a 46 year old Afro-American lawyer from Baltimore, Maryland. He was Chief Counsel for the NAACP Legal Defense and Educational Fund. His name was Thurgood Marshall and the old south had no idea what was about to happen to it.

Brown v Board of Education changed everything. Suddenly all of the pillars of the apartheid world of the American south were at risk. Integration was the law of the land. Change was in the air and fear followed. On the thought of one little white child attending school with one little black child the old south reacted loudly and, truth be told, hysterically. Virginia closed its public schools. Florida declared that federal court rulings did not apply in their state. The rise of 'segregation now, segregation forever' politicians began. All of the great and famous moments of the civil rights movement were still ahead.

All sides agreed that something momentous had happened. But what was it that *Brown* had done? I believe that what it did was to suddenly thrust into the very center of American politics a vast population of millions of people who, for all practical purposes, had simply been invisible to the white, male law makers, newspaper editors and ordinary people. The ancient custom of intentional blindness and practiced indifference could no longer hide the facts. It was no longer whites enjoying exclusively the advantages of American life. All of that was now going to be shared with 'negroes. But how, how much, where, and most important, when? Everyone suddenly had an opinion. The issue, and the people, could no longer be ignored. The invisible had become visible.

Disability, it bears saying, played no noticeable roll in any of this. At this point the United States was closing in on its two hundredth birthday and had no problem pretending race did not exist. It was simply invisible. Given the challenges of that self-deception it was easy to ignore people with intellectual and developmental disabilities. They were isolated, segregated, institutionalized, sterilized, denied education or health care, dehumanized and frightening. The one thing they were not was a part of American life.

They were, like their Afro American fellow citizens, invisible in their own land.

The United States at the beginning of the 1950s was a land of strict racial segregation. Inter-racial marriage was a crime. Voting was minimal if it happened at all. Sexual abuse of girls and women and the lynching of men and boys were an accepted truth known to all. Publically acknowledged by none. At this very moment when the country was loudly promoting itself as the greatest place on earth, the victor of a world war and center of the world there was an underbelly of apartheid as rigid as any anywhere. And it was as American as 'apple pie.'

AMERICAN HISTORY—SHORT COURSE— HOW WE GOT TO 1953

The United States of America was born when thirteen highly divergent and geographically distanced English colonies voluntarily came together as one nation. How that happened is a long story which we need to summarize briefly in order to grasp the scale of failure that came from pretending one thing and practicing another. We cannot understand the ease of marginalization of disabled people unless we know how fundamental exclusion is to the American experience from its very inception.

The colonial period began in 1607 at Jamestown, Virginia with the establishment of the first successful crown colony. In 1620 the Puritans arrived at Plymouth in what would become Massachusetts. The last of the thirteen crown colonies was Georgia which was founded in 1733. All of them were chartered by the King of England through London corporations. All were governed by different systems. Some literally were operated from London board rooms, some from on the scene London men and some, like Virginia and some New England colonies, were more or less run by democratically elected assemblies. All owned obedience to the King. They did not imagine themselves part of a single national entity but rather as individuals answerable only to themselves, their board of directors or their elected body.

Shortly after the founding of the Jamestown colony tobacco cultivation became very profitable. And with that crop came slaves. The first of them were introduced into Virginia in the early 17th Century and the practice soon became common throughout all of the southern colonies. Slaves were also owned in the north but not remotely on the scale of the south. As time passed numbers in the north declined while in the south they grew. According to the "Slave count" of 1790 there were 654,121 slaves in the south. By 1860 that number grew to 3,204,813 in the south and about 40,000 in the North, mainly in Maryland.

These colonies reflected their founding documents and their geography. Boston and the rest of New England traded with other parts of the British Empire and in doing so developed great skill as ship builders, merchants, bankers, educators etc. On the other hand the southern colonies were based on agriculture. Most of that was done by white small farmers although the economics of tobacco and later cotton made large plantations and slave labor essential. The north made money from the south with their ships while southern prosperity depended on ease of trade with England and the export import business. To the west other colonists were seeking expansion by seizure of Indian land and resources. All three happily overlooked each other's oddities. Neither gave slavery a thought. It was just the way it was.

Overtime the one thing that came to unite these independent colonies was their growing list of irritations and abuses they laid at the feet of the King and Parliament in faraway London. As the list of grievances grew so too did the tension, fear and unease. All of that came to a head in Concord, Massachusetts in April 1775 when colonial militia engaged British regulars on a patrol to seize arms.

The war of the American Revolution had begun. Gradually all of the colonies would join and increasingly, at least in the field, the colonial militias began more and more to resemble a national army. In summer 1776 delegates met in Philadelphia, Pennsylvania and signed a Declaration of Independence. Issued on July 4 it put the world on notice that what had started as a colonial squabble had grown into total war in which the colonial side intended to sever forever their ties to the British Empire.

THE COLONIES REVOLT—WHO ARE THE 'REVOLUTIONARIES?'

The war lasted eight long years and touched each of the colonies. Colonial militia, now called the Continental Army, eventually came under control of a single governmental authority. Known as the Continental Congress it was made up of delegates from each colony and had the authority to run the war. Including the responsibility of paying for it. Never successful at raising revenue the congress did agree on George Washington to be the supreme commander of the army. This was a big step for the colonies. Although soldiers for this national army would continue to come from state militias they would be, at least during a period of active service, under the command of a single officer, appointed by an elected national congress and representing the idea of a strong national presence as a single entity.

Both sides imagined invading the other. The British imagined operations from a strong base in Canada to invade the rebelling colonies. The colonials, for their part, also imagined a quick and decisive invasion of Canada. Both sides failed.

The war continued in a series of bloody but indecisive battles. Along the coast British Naval power asserted itself easily. The British were firmly able to control most of the seaports ranging from New York to Savanah. Boston changed hands a couple of times. But what the British discovered that they were unable to do was to campaign in the vast depths of the North American continent. The distances were too great, supply too long, terrain too rough and the enemy too hard to find.

In 1778 France became the first country in the world to recognize the Continental Congress as legitimate government of what, up until then, had been thirteen separate British Colonies. But diplomatic recognition was not all the American side got. France agreed to go to war with Britain and provide an entire French Army to serve under the command of General Washington. This proved to be the beginning of the end.

By the fall of 1781 the main British ground force had retreated to the Yorktown peninsula in Virginia very near the site of Jamestown. The British fleet was off in the Caribbean Sea allowing the French to grab a short but decisive naval superiority in Chesapeake Bay. When Washington's Continental Army, complete with its French regiments, arrived in Virginia the British were trapped. Unable to evacuate by sea they were forced to fight. British defenses slowly crumbled under the expertise of the French canon.

Finally, in October, the British surrendered. The American victory at Yorktown did not mark the end of the war but it did put an end to large scale military operations.

The war itself did not officially end until 1783 when the Treaty of Paris was signed. Britain recognized the independence of what was by now called The United

States of America. For the astonished victors the very real question was—we won, now what?

On the American side that meant being governed by what was called the Articles of Incorporation. Recent diplomatic and military victories had firmly planted the idea that the thirteen colonies acting in concert as one body may have some real advantages. The document itself was called a 'confederation among sovereign states.'

The Articles of Confederation set out various government responsibility. All power, authority and money however came exclusively from colonial contributions. There was no central government with real authority and, of course, it failed. Everyone agreed on that.

When the Articles of Confederation were adopted in 1781 the colonies were far from willing to give up any of their power or independence. Still national unity, however limited, was better than chaos.

When the constitutional convention convened in 1787 the question was whether or not attitudes had changed since 1781. Were the colonies, each with their own history and pride, willing to give up some of that for the advantages of a truly unified nation?

Delegates meeting to decide on a single constitution had the same thoughts when it came to giving up their privileges. "What's in it for me?" and "who belongs" in this new republic?

THE CONSTITUTIONAL CONVENTION: A NEW NATION IS BORN.

Imagine this task. You are to create a brand new country and a brand new method of governing it. The new government would have the power of war and peace, trade and commerce, courts, and many other things. It was to be structured in a way that promotes stability and limits abuse of power. It also had to reflect both the aristocratic traditions of the people about to create it but also to include the 'common people.' The ones without titles who just fought the war. They too wanted power. This is a lot to do. It does have a noble ring to it. Less so when one realizes that amongst all of this chatter about freedom, equality under the law, domestic tranquility, fairness for all, etc. all of the words are coming from only one class of people. They were all male, all white and all owners of private property. The other thing they had in common is a firm belief that the future of the world was in the hands of themselves. Rich, white, male land owners not only had the obligation but indeed the duty to govern, to lead and when necessary to control.

And this is where the story gets interesting to everyone who is not white, male, rich, property owning and now to that list we can add able bodied. Where, exactly, were we? When these founders talk about 'the people' just who do they mean? 'Freedom", "equality" and "justice" are to be created by a group of good old boys for a proposed nation made up in part of 650,000 slaves and thousands of indentured servants. How to reconcile those things was challenge enough. Needless to say people with disabilities and people who were not white were not asked their opinions. Nor were women. For whatever reasons the process unfolded and a new system of government was put into place. This government was intended to represent the interests of its founders. There was no place in it for minorities, the poor, the disabled, slaves and others.

Who were these people? These founding fathers (as they are called) who met in a sweltering summer of 1787 and succeeded in unification of thirteen previously independent states. To its new citizens it meant whatever they liked. To a South Carolina planter it meant that his life based on slavery would continue forever and that the government would limit its power but keep enough of it to get my cotton to and from the world markets. To a Connecticut fisherman it meant fair trade with New York. To a recently arrived frontiersman in Kentucky it mean a government that would support westward expansion and the conquest of native tribes. To a banker in New York it meant stability. But again all white, male property owners. The rest of us were invisible.

The delegates met in the summer of 1787. Each state had a variable number of delegates. There were fifty five in all. All white, male and owners of property. Twenty five of them were slave owners. ("The Constitution and Slavery", Univ. of Houston (2014)

To understand how Americans with all sorts of disabilities always have been, and to large degree still are, so invisible it is useful to think a bit about just what it required to be a delegate to a constitutional convention in which nearly half the members owned other human beings. Conceding that people's attitudes about slavery in general were simply different then is to excuse a pretty big flaw. The evils of slavery were not unknown to the convention. But those evils were overlooked, ignored and set aside in the universal desire to create a new nation.

To succeed in the task of nation building, particularly one proud of its lofty slogans of universal equality, justice, liberty for all, etc., it was necessary that something be ignored. After much argument and anger the delegates finally did agree on a constitution for a new nation. The operation of this newly formed United States of America depended upon stripping every semblance of human rights, dignity and personhood from African slaves laboring that hot summer in the fields of the south while their owners bargained away any hope they may have had that somehow the American Revolution would work to their benefit.

It was as if a giant wall was constructed around official reality. On the 'other' side were literally millions of people who simply became invisible. They existed, white people knew they existed, but they were separate and degraded. In order for the new country to work it was necessary to overlook them. The giant wall necessary to shield one from the reality of the slaves (and later Jim Crow) was big enough to also hide people with disabilities. Just like the African slaves disabled people were easy to just not see. And no one did see.

In spite of disability and race the delegates did come together with one purpose. To create a new government for a growing nation. General agreement had been achieved on the need to address an executive, judicial and legislative function. Out of that came our three branches of government, each with its own check and balance on the power of the other.

PRESIDENT OF THE UNITED STATES.

The first real issue to dispose of was the question of establishing a king. There was considerable support for the idea of naming George Washington the first King of the United States. When Washington very loudly and publically declared his unwillingness to consider such a thing the idea was abandoned. If no king what then?

Article Two of the constitution establishes the executive branch and describes the office of President of the United States. The President is head of state, able to negotiate (in cooperation with the Senate) treaties, grant pardons, etc. The person must be thirty five years old, native born or a citizen of the United States, (the first native born president was Martin Van Buren). Most important was that the president was to be commander in chief of the armed forces.

The establishment of such power in the hands of an executive was a question that hung heavily over the convention. A question extended to all government power including the still to be created legislative branch. Since the declaration of independence and many other documents had proclaimed the consent of the governed as the sole legitimate foundation of any sovereign state it was understood that free elections would be the method of choosing leaders. The question of just how those elections would work was one of the most difficult issues before the convention.

It must be remembered that in 1787 hereditary monarchs sat on the throws of all European governments. Only England had an elected parliament whose ultimate power was superior to that of the king. Elections were new. Particularly elections that put military power into the hands of the victor. Delegates were anxious to appear welcoming of all the men who were 'created equal' but at the same time put some serious limitations on the people's ability to elect potential candidates. This balancing act between public statements and private fears would drive the convention to some very odd choices when it came to putting power into the hands of the 'people.' The white male property owners who made up the convention were used to running the world and expected to continue doing so. Turning power over to a mob of vagabonds, ruffians, workers, etc. was the last thing they wanted. The real genius of the convention was its ability to turn inward and rely on the most extravagant democratic rhetoric in the most public places all the while limiting the real 'power of the people.' Protecting their own class from plebian populists and orators the delegates were far too busy to think of inclusion of people with disabilities or racial justice.

The first example of this fear of unlimited direct suffrage is the curious method the constitution chose to elect the president. To elect the head of state of a country the simplest method is to have votes cast and counted and the person with the most votes declared the winner. That option does not seem to have been considered. Instead more layers needed to be built in between the people power of the vote and the actual exercise of power. Power being too important to be left to the whim of voters.

It was decided that there would be a public vote for president. But what the votes actually did was elect a delegate publically committed to your candidate to a brand new institution called the Electoral College. Once every four years the college would convene by seating each of the electors chosen by popular vote. The vote of the Electoral College actually chooses the president. The electors are chosen by state. Their number dependent upon the population of the state. Thus New York has far more electors than Mississippi. What the constitutional convention did not do was to require the electors to cast their vote consistent with the popular outcome. Electors were left free to vote as they chose. Whatever the reasons pro or con that was the way it was left. If delegates just assumed the electors would follow the will of the voters they were mistaken. In less than a century later, in the election of 1876, electors went against popular will and elected a president not based on his appeal to the voters but on his willingness to broker a back room deal that smacked of everything the founding fathers hated. That flaw in the scheme plunged the United States into a century of apartheid, segregation and disgrace. A direct result of bad judgment in 1787. In their desire to protect the interests of white male property owners the founders compromised on a good many important principles. That led to success in the short run. But also triggered a series of political crisis that all festered over the question 'who belongs?'

This fear of rule by popular and unfettered vote remains a potent force in the political world. The 2014 US midterm elections being the most recent example. Election results were a huge victory for the Republican ticket that not only took control of the Senate but increased its House majority to a whopping 247 seats. 218 seats constituting a majority.

If democratic values rule one would expect that the popular vote for the House would be overwhelmingly republican. In fact the democrat candidates won 2 million more votes than their republican opponents and still lost. How can that be?

Blocking direct democracy are House rules. Each of the 435 members run for election to a particular house seat. Each seat represents about the same number of people. The House has the authority to approve the boundaries of each district. If boundaries are drawn based on some kind of rational geometric pattern the results will essentially correspond to the votes cast. But if the boundaries are redrawn in a way that gives advantage to one party by manipulating those boundaries that process is called gerrymandering. The seats in the US House are seriously gerrymandered.

The term gerrymander first entered our language in an editorial published in the Boston Gazette in 1812. It criticized the redrawing of house districts to favor the governor's party. The paper said the district looked like a salamander. The Governor's name was Elbridge Gerry. Thus the process and result of unfairly drawing district boundaries became a gerrymander. A term and practice still very much with us.

How does gerrymandering work and how does it deprive people of competitive and democratic elections? Gerrymandering succeeds by herding groups of similar voters into artificial boundaries that change the political balance of a state. Often this is done by drawing boundaries that join together communities in geographically distant and obviously separate. To visualize how this works let's look at an imaginary state called the State of Imaginary

The State of Imaginary has a population of 10 million people. Based on its population Imaginary has five seats in the US House. (Numbers are purely illustrative and not at all the ones used for apportionment). Imaginary is primarily an agricultural state, it has two large cities and is shaped like a rectangle. The two large cities are on opposite sides of the state and each has a population of about two million.

Statewide democrats hold a slight registration lead of 44% compared to 42% republican and the rest independent. But if you look at voter registration within the two large cities they are heavily democratic. If you are a republican strategist at a time when your party controls the House how can you apportion seats in a way that eliminates expensive competitive elections and at the same time guarantee your parties enduring success in future elections?

Take the first city and draw a boundary around it. That is a 'safe' democrat seat. But for the remaining four districts instead of drawing a boundary around each similar sized population block you draw them in a way that three of them have long, meandering boundaries so that they can include portions of the other large city with each portion drawing off registered democrat voters. What you end up with are republican majorities in four of the five house districts.

By visualizing our State of Imaginary you can clearly see how a party can win big majorities by carefully regulating where the votes are cast and recognizing winners not out of some majority of votes cast but rather by winners in individual house districts. No matter how contrived those districts may be. This vision pretty much describes the current districting of the House of Representatives.

Rob Rickie, writing in *The Nation* in 2015, examines the question of how democrats could have won the popular vote and lost the election so badly. He concludes that for democrats to take over the House in 2016 their popular vote plurality would need to be 10 million votes. Except perhaps under the most extraordinary of circumstance a number that is simply unrealistic.

I have dwelt on this example at some length for two reasons. It supports my point that how things really work are often vastly different than how they appear to work. Elections may be legally and fairly conducted. But what value is that if voting cannot change anything? It is the competitiveness that is missing. And without a spirit of real contest democracy just becomes a label, a vulgar formalism void of its real meaning. If it is easy to overlook this fundamental reality then it is easy to see how an issue like racism got overlooked, ignored and delayed. And if an issue of that size can be made to disappear it is very easy to see why disability is even more invisible. Who belongs continues to be the fundamental question. Are we a nation striving to include everyone? Or are we a place where only the privileged and powerful make the rules? Just for white male property owners? Or is it for everyone? The perpetual question.

    Second, the short review of how districting really works is a good opportunity to remember that the disability rights movement, along with every other progressive body, has suffered two dramatic strategic defeats recently. Defeats so damaging, that unless they are addressed, we will be at the mercy of forces not so friendly.

    The first of these recent calamities is of course what is popularly known as the "Citizen's United" case from the Supreme Court. *(Citizens United vs. Federal Election Commission.* 558 US 310. 2010).By extending what it means to be a legal person to include corporations the court also opened the way for corporate free speech rights. Just like any other person. A restriction on the amount of money that any corporation can donate to a candidate would therefore violate their corporate entity first amendment right to free speech. In other words a law attempting to regulate the amount of private money that can be spent of politics was unconstitutional. The flood gates of elections bought and sold like any other commodity are upon us. It is imperative to appreciate what a damaging thing this is. One entity, the Koch brothers, are rumored to be willing to spend $900 million of their own money on the 2016 election. Overturning the decision is perhaps the most important single issue we face. To do that will require large democratic majorities in both houses, a progressive democrat president and vacancies on the Supreme Court. In other words under a best case scenario it is many years away. No priority of survival is higher than new strategies to get us around an avalanche of money like no one has seen. Between now and the time that the right wing has bought up the last vestige of real democracy lies a window of opportunity. When it is gone it is gone forever.

The other defeat of course was the Supreme Court gutting the enforcement provisions of the Voting Rights Act. Bad law that severely undermines or enlarge the voter base and bring in more people. For a generation we enjoyed the protection of Federal Courts. We must recognize that has changed. States are now free to enact all sorts of requirements before registering voters. Registering people with disabilities and minorities has become far more difficult in the face of birth certificates, transportation issues and dozens of other 'conditions' designed to prevent the elderly, students, minorities etc. from voting. This decision turned things around completely. Instead of relying on ever expanding voter rolls we are now faced with the probability of them actually shrinking. (*Shelby County v. Holder.* 570 US 286. 2013).

THE CONGRESS—SENATE AND HOUSE OF REPRESENTATIVES.

The story of where the Senate and House of Representatives come from is illustrative of our question 'who belongs?' To create the Senate the convention had to devise a scheme with all the trappings of democracy without having to actually hold an election. But in the House the question of how many members would there be very nearly killed the new nation before it was born. In allocating seats in the new House of Representatives how, exactly, would slaves be counted? Since slaves did not enjoy any legal protections and certainly could not vote or own property they should not be counted at all according to the northern colonies. But according to the southern slave owners each slave should count as a complete person. The southern representatives having no problem arguing that this complete person was also their property and had no rights at all.

Returning to 1787...

Having agreed on a government composed of three separate branches the convention turned attention to the question of office holding. How, exactly, would these three branches of government be chosen?

THE JUDICIAL BRANCH.

The Judicial branch was easily agreed upon. Justices were to be nominated by the President and confirmed by the Senate. Appointments were to be for life.

Selecting a president and members of congress presented vastly more complicated situations that brought into conflict some of the very currents in American thought still very much with us. The power of a central government versus the rights of each of the sovereign states. Whose interests was this new government to serve? What was needed to address the central question of 'who gets power?'

Over the whole event lay the implicit understanding that whoever got power it would certainly not be non-whites, women, the poor or Native Americans. As to the people then alive with intellectual or developmental disabilities there is no record that any thought whatsoever was given to them. The notion that disabled citizens might too have a voice in government was not only unheard but was never even raised. This was to be a government of white, male property owners. And to that list we can now add ableism. A condition still very much with us.

Considering the composition of the legislative branch let us look quickly at how the Senate came about and what that event tells us about inclusion and democracy.

The thirteen colonies (now states) that sent delegates to the constitutional convention varied drastically in size and population. Small states like Rhode Island and Delaware worried that their interests would be overwhelmed by big states like New York and Pennsylvania. Sparsely populated states like South Carolina worried that they would lose influence to similarly sized but vastly more populous states such as Massachusetts.

To resolve this dilemma delegates, in what is now known as the Connecticut Compromise, abandoned both size and population and agreed that each state would have two senators. Thus states with small size and few people would enjoy equal representation in the Senate. A compromise related to the needs of its time. The desire to succeed was stronger than the desire to see that power went to people and not places.

As delegates turned their attention to how these senators would be chosen they were also thinking about just who these members were likely to be. Who were the men most capable of ruling? The more they thought about it the more the answer became clear. The best men to rule were men just like themselves.

These men were in no way typical of most males of their time. Not only were they property owners. They were also well educated and financially secure if not rich.

Surprisingly well traveled many had been to the courts of Europe. Thomas Jefferson and Benjamin Franklin had served as emissaries to France. All were aware of the French *philosophes* whose writings were radically impacting the political face of their world.

The ideas of men 'born equal' each with 'inalienable rights' were very new and most unsettling. These ideas had found their way into the declaration of independence and were by now an integral part of the nation the convention was there to invent. But they were by no means American ideas. Diderot, Voltaire, Locke, Rousseau and others poked fun at the established order and raised the possibility of much more fair and rational ways to govern. All of those ideas were known to the convention delegates.

It certainly made sense to the delegates to regard each other as equals. After all each of them was successful. Each had been on the right side of the revolutionary war. Each owned property and regarded himself as a model citizen for a new and enlightened republic. A man with a responsibility to lead.

Not mentioned but ever present was the question of the common, ordinary, uneducated, toiling, sometimes restless majority of people. Were they all to be equal partners in running this new government? Did Thomas Jefferson's fishmonger suddenly have the same standing as Jefferson himself?

These new ideas of government by democracy clearly had the down side of risking instability and mob rule. Something had to be done to protect the country from irrational lurches and chaos. While the 'people' clearly had a role in the power that could be left to a house of representatives. To guard against the rabble the Senate would be the place of wisdom, stability and tradition.

Its members would not be chosen by direct election. Instead senators were to be chosen by state legislatures. Keeping in mind that only white males could vote at all the state legislators who would be able to vote for a senate candidate would have to be men who had won local elections and if they were themselves a candidate men who were esteemed by their peers. In other words the winners would always be men just like the convention delegates. Once the senators were chosen they served a six year term. Not only were they spared a popular election but only had to return to the state legislature every sixth year for re-election. To the delegates this made sense. Stability from governance by the most qualified, the most destined, etc. The duty to govern that Rudyard Kipling would soon call 'the white man's burden.'

Unintentionally or not this scheme set up a tradition of political wheeling and dealing. Secret deals cut in what came to be known as 'smoke filled rooms.' Here cigar chomping men could gather behind closed doors, off the record, brandy in hand and decide. Once the decision was made you could go back to the public, to the floor of the legislature, etc. and go through a charade of votes, speeches etc. But the real decisions were made in an environment of 'horse trading', deals, bribes, threats, promises and advancement. It was not democracy but it was stability and perpetual governance by the same class of man.

Obviously the poor were not to be included in this selection. The selection was all about excluding people. No one represented Native Americans or the millions of slaves. The absurd notion that women could vote had not yet been suggested and certainly no one represented the interests of females.

People with disabilities were simply not thought of at all. To make this scheme work and call it democracy every person not a white male property owner had to become invisible. Topping that list of invisible people were those with intellectual and developmental disabilities.

This plan for election of senators was followed until the seventeenth amendment was adopted in 1913. Since then they are elected by direct vote. But the tradition of behind the scenes manipulation became as much a part of political life as kissing babies. This was a convention of white male property owners who sat down with people just like them and tried to solve problems in the world they occupied.

A world that did not include people with disabilities. It didn't even include women White people only of course. The kinds of practices we have come to think of as inclusive were not so much rejected by the convention as simply not considered. A political precedent was set that created the habit of simply ignoring certain things. Race, as we shall see, being one. But disability and poverty are two others, less known perhaps, but equally invisible. All would play significant roles in the future and in far more jarring ways then would have been required had they been included in the first place. To claim 'all men are created equal' simply meant not seeing, thinking about or in any way acknowledging millions of people.

Having settled on a senate the convention now turned its attention to the other part of the legislative branch. The United States House of Representatives, it was decided, would be directly elected by the people. Its term of office was intentionally set at two years to assure mixing with voters. Taxation having been a major cause of the revolution it was decided that all revenue bills must originate here in the "people's House." Unlike the Connecticut compromise which addressed the representational issue of the size of a state (remember that each state got two regardless of population) seats in the House would be assigned based on a state's population. States with more people simply got more power in the House. This sounds simple. But the details of what 'deals' had to be made to achieve a superficial appearance of unity make up an amazing part of the story. For people with disabilities the decision to count only a part of a person and not a whole human was to have long reaching ramifications in political thought for centuries. Intentional or not the idea that anything can be compromised and that only the strong participate became engrained in US thought and practice.

How to decide how many representatives a state would get? The more people the more representation. The fewer the people the less the representation. How could states with small populations feel confident that they are properly represented? Who gets counted?

This is revisiting the same big state—small state issue they had resolved in the Senate in favor of geography over people. The southern states, regardless of size, were mostly agrarian economies composed of a few cities and thousands of small homesteads. Their total population was vastly lower than the more industrial and developed north. If population were to be the sole criteria for seats in the House the underpopulated states would lose even more voice and power in this new government.

The south was desperate to avoid losing power. The north was desperate to not see the convention come undone. To appreciate their problem imagine a southern state. The state has a population of 100 freemen. It also has 100 slaves. Is there a way to pretend the state's population is 160 and do so in a way that grants absolutely no rights, benefits or citizenship to the slaves? It turns out that the answer is yes. For the north such an outcome could be claimed as a victory. Not counting slaves had been an important position to the north but not counting them all was what it settled for. To the south the agreement meant their power position in the new country went way up while changing nothing in their home states. What could be wrong? The delegates placed their hopes on believing that nothing could go wrong. And on the principle that a human being is only three fifths of a person the new nation was born.

Enter the Three Fifths Compromise. The best example I know of for 'kick the can down the road' politics. By that I mean if there is a serious problem one way to handle it is to delay its resolution to a future time. No matter how fundamental a dispute there is always a way to put it off. By agreeing to an apportionment scheme that intentionally skirted the ever percolating issues of slavery and race they basically 'punted' a real solution.

All this to shed light on our inquiry as to why people with intellectual disabilities are so easily undervalued and simply not seen. Our community has a lot in common with the slaves in our apportionment story. No one there to advocate for, represent, include or, indeed, even think about a huge number of people. We were not at the table. Neither were the slaves. Neither of us mattered one wit.

All of these matters aside the convention finished its work and submitted the proposed constitution to the states for ratification. It was agreed that when nine states ratified the document all thirteen would be bound by it and it could go into effect.

The document itself reflected the men who created it. It proposed three separate but equal branches of government that became the model for democratic structures worldwide. On paper it appeared to be the most egalitarian government imaginable. But a closer reading revealed that whatever the appearance of governing may be its decisions would continue to be made just like the men who wrote the document.

The Executive branch created the office of the Presidency. Into those hands went the awesome power of being commander and chief of the armed forces as well as head of state and chief executive. Elections were to be held but after they were over the real power lay in the hands of an electoral college appointed by the states. If things went bad in an election and the wrong kind of person won that could be fixed in the Electoral College without forfeiting privileges to the whim of popular vote.

The Judicial branch was to consist of a Supreme Court and lower courts as decided by Congress. Justices to the Supreme Court would be appointed for life (to avoid popular pressure) but first must be nominated by the President and confirmed by a vote of the Senate. Senators, people just like the drafters, thus retained the power to control appointment to the Supreme Court.

The legislative branch would consist of two houses: the House of Representatives and the Senate. Each would have their own constitutional duties and powers. The Senate would be appointed by professional politicians in state legislatures making sure that at least one of the legislative bodies was immune from popular vote. The House membership would be based on the population of the state and elected by direct vote. But of course that included counting slaves as three fifths of a person and not allocating them one recognized right under the law.

THE NEW NATION BEGINS.

With the issues of race, poverty and disability (among others) left totally of the picture. On June 21, 1789 the state of New Hampshire became the ninth state to ratify the constitution and on March 4, 1789 the new nation was up and running.

At least as many questions remained as answers provided. Political compromise had made the nation possible but also lead to some serious contradictions that were bound, sooner or later, to cause lots of problems. And they did. And it was way sooner than later.

George Washington was elected the first president. Even he was unable to serve two terms as president without the founding contradictions of federal supremacy and race coming to the fore and leaving their mark on his administration.

The first was the issue of the power of the federal government pitted against the rights of the individual states. The new government of course needed revenue and one method of raising it by prompt Congressional approval of a federal tax on 'spirits.' This was a time where people drank a lot of whiskey. Because it is relatively easy to distill it was produced and sold in huge quantities. To the people of the backcountry the idea of paying more for their whiskey because some far away government in

Washington, DC said they had to smacked of tyranny. Most distilleries simply refused to pay.

President Washington pleaded, cajoled and threatened but nothing changed. The states refused to collect the taxes and the federal law was in danger of being shown to be meaningless. Finally Washington sent a specially empowered 'emissary' with the authority to collect the taxes. Local people in Western Pennsylvania responded by putting an army of five hundred armed men into the field and laying siege to the fortified home of the tax 'emissary.'

In 1794, by appealing to state governors, Washington managed to amass what amounted to a federal armed force composed of militias from various states. This force of thirteen thousand was sent west with orders to put down any rebellion and collect the taxes. Before the federal army arrived the insurgents gave up and went home. This time the persistent rub between federal or state power did not quite come to violence. But it was a close call. For the moment it seemed settled that federal power was supreme. Nothing was actually settled. But like so many other issues of the day everyone pretended that they had been. (Slaughter, Thomas. P. *The Whiskey Rebellion: Frontier Epilogue to the American Revolution.* Oxford. 1986).

Race also played a role in Washington's presidency. The old colonies, now the new states, were rigidly slave states or not. Slave states treated slaves simply as property. An increasing number of free-state people were more likely to see a runaway slave as a sympathetic fellow human. Some free states honored requests from their southern countrymen to please return out property. Some did not.

Southern outrage over runaway slaves lead to the first Fugitive Slave Law. Signed by President Washington in 1793 it required people to return runaway slaves to their rightful owners under penalty of a $500 fine or possible imprisonment. By signing the law Washington placated the south by sacrificing the slaves but also strengthened the hand of a strong central government. One that had the authority to collect taxes and return runaway slaves. (Annals of Congress. Second Congress. Second Session. Nov. 5, 1792-March 2, 1793. Pages 1414-1415).

Most US citizens are aware of Mt. Vernon the quaint colonial mansion a short boat ride south of Washington, DC. As the home of the first president it has become both a national shrine and tourist attraction of the first order. Fewer are aware that when Washington lived there it was a thriving southern plantation totally dependent on slave labor. Washington himself owned slaves all of his life.

The nation was founded on a principle of blindness toward the very existence of millions of people. Washington was just one who could not see or had convinced himself not to see that all the high sounding language of equality the nation claimed as its birthright could not change the real world.

All the privileges formed on the backs of slaves could not erase the slaves. Whether or not Washington and others chose to see them or not they were real. Racism was real. Abelism was real. Sexism was real. The white male property owners who founded the country expected to benefit and they did. The rest not so much.

During Washington's administrations the national capital was first in New York City and later Philadelphia. The decision to locate it on a worthless piece of swamp land between Maryland and Virginia had been made and what would be called the District of Columbia was being transformed. It was not yet called Washington, DC.

When the Washington family moved to Philadelphia they brought with them over a dozen slaves. Since Pennsylvania was a free state it was a bit awkward what with a Fugitive Slave Law and all. But all the other southern gentlemen brought their slaves too and business went on as usual.

Washington had one embarrassing moment regarding his slaves when one of them ran away. In 1796 a twenty two year old woman named Ona Judge left when she found out that Martha, the First Lady, was going to give her away as a wedding present. To the south a runaway slave was a scandal and a crime. They looked to Washington, as one of them, to find and vigorously punish. To the north the story rather showed the utter cruelty of slavery. It drove new wedges between the two parties. Distrust grew along with an unease that the compromises they all made to form a country may not be over and done with after all. In the end Ona Judge was returned. No record of punishment exists. ("George Washington, Slave Catcher", New York Times, Feb. 16. 2015).

On December 14, 1799, a few weeks before a new century, George Washington, the Father of His Country, died. A period of national mourning and commemoration began and, in many ways, has never ended.

What the slaves at Mt. Vernon thought at the passing of Master George is not known. At the time of his death three hundred eighteen slaves are known to have lived there although likely not all of them belonged to him.

Around the man grew great mythic stories of genius, glory, humility, etc. What is fact and what is not lost to the ages. One thing we do know is that the two myths so often associated with George Washington are not true. He did not cut down a cherry tree. He did not have wooden teeth. He did have lifelong dental issues and he did have dentures. Said to be life like he was so pleased he actually had several pairs.

The dentures should have looked good. They were made from teeth pulled from the mouths of his slaves. ("Washington Took His Slaves Teeth, Freedom Rider (2004) retrieved from internet February 17, 2015.

ADAMS/JEFFERSON—POLITICAL POLARITY, A SUDDEN EXPANSION AND THE NEED FOR MORE COMPROMISE.

George Washington was elected president in 1788 and 1792. It was understood that Washington was really running unopposed. At the time whatever candidate came in second became vice president. An odd scheme that lasted until the ratification of the twelfth amendment in 1804 required the Electoral College to elect a president and vice president running as a team.

The issue became acute in 1800 when Jefferson's most bitter political foe, Aaron Burr, became his vice president. Burr ran off to New Orleans where he tried to engineer the secession of the western states. He was tried and found not guilty of treason but became even more of a problem when in 1804 he killed revolutionary war hero and Washington's secretary of the Treasury Alexander Hamilton in a duel

The system was what it was and due to oddity in the Electoral College Washington was elected in 1788 with 69 votes, independents got 35 votes and John Adams 34. Adams became vice president. In 1792 Washington was elected unanimously by the Electoral College and Adams remained vice president.

Thus the hotly contested election of 1800 was the first bitterly fought one. Adams ran on the Federalist ticket. His party wanted a strong federal government in order, in part, to restrain the popular excess feared from voting. Adams was from Boston and looked to the world for trade, for the profitable business of ship building and the need to control oceanic trade routes. Adams was elected President with 71 electoral votes. Jefferson came in second (becoming his rivals vice president) with 68 electoral votes. But what do those electoral votes mean in terms of democratic participation? (Ferling, Thomas. *Adams v Jefferson: The Tumultuous of 1800*. Oxford University. 2004.)

Thomas Jefferson on the other hand was from tidewater Virginia. On his estate of Monticello lived the six hundred slaves that he owned. (Jefferson/Monticello web site, retrieved Feb 23, 2015). Jefferson ran on the Democratic Party ticket arguing the need for a reduced federal power and a vision of a more direct democracy by governing primarily through the states. As an agrarian farmer, slave holder and business person Jefferson's political posture in 1800 was to look inward and find the country's future in the west. He and Adams count not have disagreed more. Burr had also adopted the mantel of the Democratic Party and in the election of 1804 he and Jefferson tied in the Electoral College with 73 votes. Adams and his running mate Thomas Pickney received 65 and 64 respectfully.

At this point the new country had held three presidential elections. It is a good time to look at just who voted. If my thesis that the most American of founding principles is exclusion that should be showing up by now.

In 1800 the population of the United States was about 5.3 million. About a million were slaves. About a million were white males and the rest were 'other.' The figures from the Adams/Jefferson race in 1796 are illustrative.

Adams was elected President with 71 electoral votes. Jefferson came in second (becoming his rivals vice president) with 68 electoral votes. But what do those electoral votes mean in terms of democratic participation?

John Adams was elected President with a popular vote of 35,726. (National Archives) Out of a population of 5.3 million only .006604% of the population could elect the president. All others were ineligible.

Total votes cast in 1796 added up to about 1% of the population. 99% had no voice at all and if they had the Electoral College was not bound by the popular vote. Is it any wonder that not a thought was given to people with a disability?

Dorothea Dix would not found the first institution until 1848. Until then virtually no record exists of people with disabilities playing any roll in or being thought of as a full participant in US life. Officially we did not exist. US politics rolled on as the exclusive property of white male property owners. No one else mattered.

By now we see an emerging pattern of two political issues that have repeated themselves countless times over the life of the country. These issues *are* United States politics. Squeezed between them is the real question of 'who belongs'?

People with disabilities are captured between these twin issues just like everyone else. 'Who belongs' is, after all, the central question for people with disabilities.

Caught between two titans like federalism and myopia how have people with disabilities fared? When do we finally appear in this story? What is required of us to gain full membership? What do we do now? As this story continues to unfold we will see recognizable patterns appear again and again. Sometimes these patterns are good and sometimes bad. Where are examples of disabled interests truly prevailing? What about nondisabled interests? When were we present? When were we invisible?

The first of these titans is, of course, federal power versus state's rights. When thirteen colonies came together to form a new nation they did so voluntarily. Each of them represented a sovereign entity.

All of them were proud of their independence and unique culture and economy. At the same time they recognized that divided they were likely too small and weak to survive for long. When these colonies finally came together in one union each of them voluntarily gave up a certain amount of power to the newly created federal government. Just how much of their power they gave up has been a subject of passionate disagreement ever since.

The new country very nearly came apart over the relatively simple issue of acquiring additional territory. The constitution's drafters exhausted themselves compromising over slavery in order to secure agreement. No thought or guidance was given on the question of what to do about slaves in the event the country grew. If you believed in the supremacy of state's rights then it followed that each new state should be free to decide for themselves about slavery. But since more slave states meant more power if you were a federalist it followed that an issue of such importance was a federal one to be decided by the nationally elected Congress. That same polarity is with us today. (Medicaid expansion is an example).

With the implementation of the Affordable Cars Act states are free to accept or reject an expansion of Medicaid funding to pay for in home care among other things. Quite predictably we see states whose leaders believe there is a federal roll to be played in health care. By accepting the expansion and they are vastly expanding the number of their citizens who are insured.

States that have refused Medicaid expansion do so behind a state's rights argument that says the federal government has no role to play in health care. Expansion is equated with a federal over reach of authority. By appealing to an anti-federalist view these states put the importance of the principle over the health care needs of their own people. No need to argue against health care. You just need to argue in favor of state's rights. A principle so strong as to very nearly tear the new country apart in 1820. There are times where it seems destined to do the same today. Quite often it feels as if nothing has changed.

In 1796 John Adams defeated Thomas Jefferson by a narrow margin. It had been the country's first contentious election with both candidates clearly stating very different views. Adams, the federalist, favored development of population centers, fortifications, and a vigorous shipping industry out of his native Boston. All of which was to be promoted and watched over by a strong central government. Jefferson, the Virginia gentlemen and plantation owner, could not have been more different. He believed the country to be essentially agrarian and would prosper from local control through state government with its eyes to the west.

But it would be the election of 1800 remembered both for its animosity and unexpected outcome. During his four years in office Adams had followed federalist principles. Although they look minor now his policies opened him up to attack from Jefferson as a power hungry big government spender from New England. Adams, according to Jefferson, had abused state's rights.

Disability rights strategist do well to look closely at this election for a number of reasons. Contemporary issues aside the election was decided by application of compromise solutions left over from the constitutional convention. The first was Jefferson's skillful use of state's rights to frighten voters into fear of a federal tyranny. The second was the application of the three-fifths compromise. By counting slaves Jefferson was barely able to prevail. Had slaves not been counted Adams would have won.

And finally it was the new nation's introduction to the phenomena of a hotly contested campaign turning on a few issues into the victor promptly changing his mind on most everything and implementing as policy all the things the 'people' just thought they had voted against.

Adams had done a number of things (Alien and Sedition Act, a near war with France among others) but national defense policy was what made him vulnerable to Jefferson's endless attacks. During Washington's administration Congress had authorized the construction of first class ships of the line to strengthen the nearly non-existent United States Navy. Although the frigates (as they are called) were ordered before his election they came on line during Adams' presidency.

The first of these was the USS Chesapeake with thirty-eight guns. The second, the USS Constitution, was even bigger with forty-four guns. By contemporary standards these were enormous war ships. It was not difficult for a candidate to convince the voters of the agrarian west and south, most of which were small farmers and tradesmen, that these giant ships, enriching the ports of New England with their tax dollars, were unnecessary, dangerous, expensive and the direct result of federal usurpation of power. The first time that The Tyranny in Washington worked.

Jefferson jumped right on the issue. His campaign was all about his devotion to small government, fiscal restraint, and popular democracy. In one of his rare campaign documents he wrote and distributed widely "I shall be most chagrined if we do not immediately lay up the whole fleet." (Adams, Henry, *"History of the United States during the Administrations of Thomas Jefferson"*, pg. 151, Library of America (1986)).

Jefferson was elected with 73 electoral votes to Adams 65. Popular vote results were Jefferson 41,330 to 25,952 for Adams. On March 4, 1801 Thomas Jefferson, the great champion of small government and limited federal power, was sworn in as the third President of the United States.

As one of his first acts the new president changed his mind on the frigates. In fact he liked them so much he ordered more. In 1803 he order the USS Constitution on a combat mission to the Mediterranean Sea where the crew promptly mutinied for lack of payment. Exposing to Jefferson's embarrassment another chronic problem; shortage of cash.

In 1776 Jefferson had been the principle drafter of the Declaration of Independence. By the time he became president the world had changed in ways quite unimaginable in 1776. The first of these of course was the success of the very revolution Jefferson had aided in. It was a shock that a group of thirteen small colonies isolated along the seashore of a vast and unexplored continent has wrested independence from the world's greatest power.

Perhaps more significant was the French revolution that not only established a new form of government but toppled a centuries old divine right monarchy; for good measure the revolution beheaded its last king. A series of governments by committee, by junta, by military rule, etc. followed until, in November, 1799 the National Assembly was overthrown by a junta that included a very young Napoleon Bonaparte. In October 1800 the French people voted Napoleon First Counsel for Life. (Roberts, Andrew. *Napoleon: A Life.* Penguin. 2014.)

In 1804 Napoleon crushed the allied army sent against him at the Battle of Austerlitz. The victory left him absolute master of continental Europe. But that same year his Navy was wiped out at the Battle of Trafalgar. In December he was crowned Emperor Napoleon I. In only a few decades France had gone from being an absolute monarchy to denouncing all kings only to be ruled by a hereditary Emperor.

By now the new Emperor had acquired enemies near and far. Russia was not subdued. England was safe behind its fleet. There were two things Napoleon knew; one was the he did not need any more diversions and the other is that he was broke.

Whatever the details the new French emperor and the old American revolutionary now agreed on a monumental deal that would eliminate a distraction for Napoleon as well as allow him to acquire the cash to continue his wars. For Jefferson it was a deal that more than doubled the size of the country. Without asking Congress Jefferson 'bought' Louisiana from France. Whatever exactly Louisiana may be. No one knew for sure. But what lay ahead very nearly destroyed the fragile union. Once again the unseen and forgotten (in this case slaves) and the differences over states' rights would rise and impact the best of intentions in unforeseen ways.

Slavery, that unresolved and seemingly invisible monster, shaped the country is countless ways. Some we have seen and others we will soon visit. But it is well to here remember that westward expansion of the United States would not have been possible without a dramatic intervention by slaves. In this case the great Haiti Slave Rebellion.

Regarded as the most successful slave rebellion the one on Haiti began in 1791 and ended in 1804 with the islands complete independence. The French revolutionary government had abolished slavery in France in 1794. Reluctantly the abolition was applied to the colonies of France as well but was not followed entirely. On Haiti a young self-educated former slave named Toussaint L'Ouverture was one of many slaves who believed the French were about to reinstitute slavery. Under his leadership an armed rebellion broke out which engulfed the entire island, lead to the return of slavery and ultimately cost the lives of at least 55,000 French soldiers, 100,000 islanders and became a grave yard for additional Napoleonic troops sent to suppress the revolt. Napoleon, fed up with western hemisphere politics, simply decided to get rid of it by withdrawing and, in his eyes, withdrawing with the additional benefit of lots of cash from the sale of a distant and not very desirable place called Louisiana. Without the slave rebellion on Haiti there would have been no Louisiana Purchase. (James, C.L.R. *The Black Jacobins: Toussaint L'Ouverture and the Santo Domingo Revolt.* Vintage. 1969).

THE LOUISIANA PURCHASE—SLAVERY, STATES RIGHTS' AND NEAR CALAMITY.

Ambassadors were sent to Paris to negotiate a possible purchase of the city of New Orleans only. They were surprised when in mid-April 1803 the French asked if they would be interested in all of the Louisiana territory. The delegates moved quickly and by May had agreed to purchase 828,000,000 square miles for the price of three cents an acre.

The territory was enormous. Its actual boundaries were in some cases unknown and imprecise. What was known was that it stretched from the Mississippi River in the east all the way to the Rocky Mountains in the west. It began at the Gulf of Mexico in the south and extended to the Canadian border in the north. What was not known was that this territory would eventually include all of part of fifteen states. In December 1803 the last French officials left New Orleans. Hastily or not Thomas Jefferson had just doubled the size of the new country. The Louisiana Territory was now a sovereign part of the United States of America. (Forbes, Robert Pierce. *The Missouri Compromise and Its Aftermath: Slavery and the Meaning of America.* Univ. of North Carolina. 2009.)

Jefferson's first consideration was sending a corps of exploration into the remote northwest regions and report on land, resources, climate and particularly Indians. Meriwether Lewis, Jefferson's personal secretary was named a leader and the famous Lewis and Clark expedition eventually extended additional claims all the way to the mouth of the Columbia River on the far off Pacific Ocean.

Interesting to note what instructions they carried regarding the natives. Their first priority was to avoid hostilities. The second was to gain as much intelligence as possible about tribal size, power, etc. No thought was given to the independent native nations. No one considered for a moment negotiating as equals. Native people enjoyed no recognition beyond submission. Not for the first time were Native Americans lumped into the category of the unseen, unrecognized and uncounted. But they became as invisible as the disabled. As annoying as slavery. As politically powerless as women. As forgotten as the poor.

It did not take long for slavery to sidetrack any euphoria about expansion. If the nation were to move to the west that inevitably would mean new states. And would those states be Free states or slave states? Upon that question lay the balance of power in Congress. It quickly became the biggest question of the day and very nearly ended the unity of the new country.

By 1820 the question of slavery in the new lands was tearing at the fabric of the union. That year Alabama was admitted to the union as slave state. This brought into balance the number of states on both sides. In addition the southern states were worried that there was a plan afoot to make what was then a part of northern Massachusetts into a new free state called Maine. If that were true the south wanted Missouri admitted as a slave state.

In what came to be known as the Missouri Compromise it was agreed that slavery was to be prohibited in the former Louisiana Territory north of a parallel line that aligns on modern maps with the northern border of Arkansas and the tip of the Texas panhandle. The State of Missouri which, although north of the line, would be allowed to be admitted as a slave state. Agreement in hand Congress adopted the compromise and admitted Maine as a free state.

The compromises of the constitutional convention continued time and again to force politicians to simply keep putting resolution off in favor of more and more convoluted compromises. As time passed the exclusion Afro Americans, women, the disabled and poor, becomes less and less a stability issue and more and more one of survival. Without full inclusion of everyone what did the future hold?

The Missouri Compromise held the fragile union, now strung together precariously by a balance of Free states and slave states, together for a few years. But its delicate balance would soon be overcome by unforeseen developments that would soon change everything. Once again the nation nearly came undone as a direct result of the compromises of the constitutional convention. To create the union it had been necessary to overlook the existence of millions of people of whom slaves were merely the most numerous and obvious. It was becoming harder and harder to pretend that so many people played no role in the republic.

In 1824 the Republic of Mexico established its first constitution and all of what is now the State of Texas was the sovereign territory of Mexico. To the government in Mexico City the distant plains of Texas were not only part of Mexico but a very sparsely settled part as well. The Mexican government adopted immigration policies that encouraged people from the United States to immigrate to Texas, become Mexican citizens and settle the land.

But to the thousands of new settlers the Mexican government seemed distant, hostile and deaf to their desires. By 1835 the issue of the rights of immigrants in Texas became violent and volunteers from the United States swarmed to Texas and soon overwhelmed the small Mexican garrisons.

Alarmed by the violence and anti-Mexican behavior President Santa Anna mobilized an army and invaded Texas in mid-February, 1836. The fighting was violent but inconclusive. Even though Santa Anna's army defeated the Texans at Goliad and slaughtered the defenders of the Alamo the war continued. The army of Texas, now under the command of Sam Houston, simply moved further and further to the east ahead of the pursuing Mexicans. In frustration Santa Anna split his forces and he and the main body were surprised by Houston's attack on April 21, 1836. This battle of San Jacinto lead to Santa Anna's capture and ultimately to the withdrawal of the Mexican Army. Texas had declared its independence back in March of 1836 and now, with the Mexican army defeated, declared the war won and went on with the process of nation building. Mexico, however humiliated, refused to recognize Texas independence. (Nofi, Alber A. *The Alamo and the Texas War for Independence.* Da Capo Press. 2001).

After a decade of independence Texas was admitted to the union as a slave state on December 29, 1845. Suddenly the delicate balance of power was altered in favor of slavery and the effectiveness of the Missouri Compromise no longer relevant. The north, frantic to maintain the balance admitted Iowa on December 28, 1846 and Wisconsin in May of 1848. The key issue continued to be slavery; that seemingly unresolvable elephant in the room bequeathed by the compromises of 1790.

Unforeseen in all of this was war with Mexico. A war that once again would alter the map of both countries and plunge the nation into another crisis threatening its very survival.

THE MEXICAN WAR, MORE COMPROMISE AND VIOLENCE.

Texas was now a part of the United States. But just what constituted Texas was unclear and highly disputed. The now defunct Republic of Texas claimed its western border to be the Rio Grande River. Mexico did not recognize that claim and insisted that Texas ended at the Nueces River further east. Tension in the disputed territory, which included hostile Indians who insisted neither side had any claim on their territory, continued in both fury and determination. Santa Anna, politically recovered from the debacle at San Jacinto, sent an army to northern Mexico. In return United States president James K. Polk sent 3,500 soldiers to the Nueces River. Both armies eyed each other warily and small but violent clashes occurred.

Exactly what happened in the disputed territory during the late winter and early spring of 1845 is still not clear. The United States claimed Mexican soldiers had crossed the Rio Grande into what from the Mexican viewpoint were simply maneuvers in their own country but on the United States side was an invasion. Or at least so we claimed. What mattered was how it was characterized and President Polk made his position clear when he wrote Congress "Mexico has passed the boundary of the US, has invaded out territory and shed American blood on American soil." (Bauer, Jack K. *"The Mexican War",* Univ. of Nebraska Press, (1974)). On May 13, 1846 Congress declared war on Mexico.

The reasons for going to war were far from convincing to a large segment of the public. Members of Congress, led by former president John Quincy Adams, strongly opposed it. The Whig party feared expansion of slavery into any new territory. For their part the southern members were delighted. Regional tensions ran high as illustrated by an obscure Congressman from Illinois named Abraham Lincoln.

Lincoln was a rising member of the Whig party and demanded to be shown the exact spot where Mexican troops had violated US territory. His objections were voted down and the highly divided nation went to war.

US settlers had immigrated to the Mexican territory of California in numbers large enough to surpass native Mexicans. President Polk had ordered a US military expedition to map and claim portions of the Oregon territory and upon the opening of hostilities with Mexico John C. Fremont moved his troops to San Francisco. After a short time of huffing and puffing the territory, under threat of military action, declared itself and independent nation but was hastily admitted to the union in December 1846 as a free state. The north rejoiced. The south seethed.

Meanwhile back at the disputed Texas border the US Army launched an invasion of Northern Mexico. Mexican resistance was fierce and both sides suffered heavy casualties in the battle for the city of Monterrey. The northern theater of war became a stalemate.

In 1847 the US launched an enormous armada of war ships from Corpus Christi and New Orleans. Under the command of General Winfield Scott they landed south of the city of Vera Cruz on March 9, 1847. Naval guns were removed from the war ships and soon bombarded the defenders of Vera Cruz into submission.

From there Scott launched an overland campaign against Mexico City which fell to US forces on September 6 after a desperate and bloody resistance. The Mexican government had fled so there was no one to formally surrender. Nevertheless with the fall of its capital and its northern provinces occupied by US forces Mexico had been effectively and decisively defeated.

In the early months of 1848 US and representatives of a newly formed Mexican government met to discuss peace terms. The result was the treaty of Guadalupe Hidalgo (February 2, 1848). The US agreed to contribute several million dollars towards Mexico's debt. In return the US got territory that constituted all of present day California, Nevada, Utah, New Mexico and parts of Texas, Oklahoma, Kansas and Wyoming. (See Bauer, K. Jack, *The Mexican War, 1846-1848,* Univ. of Nebraska Press (1974)).

Rejoicing in the US was short as slave states and free states jockeyed desperately over the question of slavery in the new lands. Once again the old issue of compromise of slavery that made the success of the constitutional convention possible reared its head and again threatened the very existence of the nation.

In June of 1850 representatives of nine slave states met in Nashville to discuss succeeding from the union and forming their own slave owning nation. More moderate voices prevailed but it was a closely run thing.

Under the leadership of Henry Clay of Kentucky Congress went to work on what came to be known as the Compromise of 1850. Again both sides gave up something but managed to preserve at least the appearance of a united country. Texas had claimed New Mexico as part of her territory and by the compromise abandoned that notion. The border of the Texas panhandle was set in conformity with the line adopted in the compromise of 1820. California was confirmed as a free state. Slavery in the District of Columbia was abolished and the territories of Utah and New Mexico were allowed to vote on slavery. No slavery was to be allowed in the Arizona territory. (Remini, Robert V. *At the Edge of the Precipice:*

Henry Clay and the Compromise that Saved the Union. Basic Books. 2010).

As we have seen before this compromise was necessary because the flaws in the original constitutional scheme appeared again. What was the role of the states? Did the federal government have power to ban slavery? No thought was given to the Native population or the Mexican settlers that had been in the southwest for centuries. And, as always, the wishes of people with disabilities were not remotely considered. Thus the expanded but bitterly divided nation stumbled ahead through a few more years of uneasy Union.

The Compromise of 1850 is a good place to look back at the great three/fifths compromise of sixty years before. White, male property owners so loved the idea of joining together into a great nation that they had agreed to do so by purposefully overlooking the humanity of millions of people. For the northerner property meant land, canals, factories, ships, companies of all kinds. For the southerner property meant the ownership of other men. Both agreed that they had a nearly divine right to the ownership of their property which was to be used exclusively for their pleasure, whim and profit. Upon that much they agreed. And upon that agreement rested the union.

So desperate were these property owning men that the northerners even went along with passage of what was called The Fugitive Slave Act. Enacted as a part of the Compromise of 1850 the law required that any run-away slave found in a free state be returned to his or her owner. Failure to cooperate was punishable with imprisonment and fine. Northerners promptly labeled it the "Bloodhound Law".

It is curious that the south, both then and now, closely associated with the notion of states' and limitation of federal power, would use just that federal authority without apology when it resulted in something they wanted. If it took federal authority to secure the return of run-away slaves then so be it. With the political world turned on its head by this reversal of state rights the northern states began to use the old southern term 'nullification.' State legislatures simply declared federal laws to not apply in their jurisdiction.

To further alienate the south Harriett Beecher Stowe wrote "Uncle Tom's Cabin" the same year the Fugitive Slave Act became law. It became an international best seller literally over-night. To the great annoyance of the south.

In response to the act Harriet Tubman ran her famous underground railroad. In defiance of the law northerners hid, aided, assisted and protected as many as 60,000 escaped slaves. The south seethed.

Dred Scott had been born a slave and in a series of sales and movement had accompanied his owner to a number of free-states. Scott had been left alone in some of those states. Scott asserted that he was free because of his residency in states where slavery was a crime. In a dispute that does not concern us Scott filed a law suit asking a federal court in Missouri to declare him a free man and not subject to a demand for his return to the widow of his late owner. The legal dispute wrangled their way through the courts for nearly a decade and finally reached the United States Supreme Court.

On March 6, 1857 the court handed down the most famous or infamous decision of the era. It was called Scott v. Sanford. The sweeping decision not only played a major role in developments but tells us a lot about how those twin issues of state rights and invisible problems came home to roost. For people with disabilities the decision is both appalling and instructive.

First the court ruled in favor of state rights and declared portions of the Missouri Compromise unconstitutional by finding that Congress had no authority to decide on slavery in the territories. But it is their characterization of Dred Scott that illustrates the point I have made over and over. That the flawed original compromises set a precedent for the nation to proceed with business as usual all the while ignoring the very existence of large numbers of people. Slaves being one. The disabled, who were present through all of this, were another. The court ruled that it was unconstitutional for anyone but a white person to be a citizen. The fact that Scott had lived in free-states, offered to buy his freedom, etc. mattered not. The court simply held that because of his race he could never be a citizen or have any legal standing and was therefore barred from seeking redress in federal court.

For the first time in its history the court ruled that millions of human beings living within its jurisdiction simply had no legal existence. They were non-persons. They could never hope to assert any rights whatsoever. They were invisible. And if a country can overlook millions of slaves it was very easy to overlook people with disabilities. Like the slaves they had no legal rights or recognition.

Thus, for the African slave the idea of some kind of inclusion simply did not apply. The union was based on a fiction. And as time passed that fiction returned time and again to nearly tear the young nation apart. Whenever a crisis had arisen Congress, unable or unwilling to address the real issue, simply found a compromise both sides disliked but continued to live with. This one, in 1850, seemed to solve the immediate problem. That illusion last four years.

In 1854 Congress enacted the Kansas-Nebraska Act. As populations and territories began to form in the newly acquired land they brought with them the same old question. Would they be admitted to statehood as free or slave? And once again Congress, unable or unwilling to decide, compromised by allowing the residents of the new states to decide by popular vote. (Wunder. John R. *The Nebraska-Kansas Act of 1854.* Univ. of Nebraska. 2009).

Although Missouri had been admitted as a free state slavery had been widely practiced and, for the first time, with little success. The Missouri climate meant that several months a year it was simply too cold to grow crops. During those winter months the slaves still had to be fed. A slave not working is a slave not profitable. Slowly slavery receded from Missouri.

The climate related issues in Missouri made it a certainty that no one would seriously try to admit Nebraska as a slave state. With both sides equally balanced they turned their attention to one place only. The Territory of Kansas.

Kansas was the next big prize in the power struggle between north and south and now both sides hastened to send settlers. Some kind of election would decide free or slave and in their enthusiasm to influence the vote both sides turned Kansas into a virtual proxy war for their wishes.

The two antagonistic groups of settlers were informally divided into camps referred to as 'free-soil' for the anti-slavery settlers and 'border ruffians' for the pro-slavery faction. In 1855 a large number of border ruffians crossed the border from Missouri and set up a hastily formed territorial legislature. They held elections on the spot and formed a territorial government in which 37 of the 39 legislative seats were held by pro-slavery members.

Not to be out maneuvered the Free soil faction petitioned Congress to overturn the election on the grounds that the people who voted were not 'residents' of Kansas. In other words they alleged voter fraud. Evidence in support of this objection was overwhelming but Congress was not anxious to make a call and thereby set themselves up for blame. Instead they appointed a commission that went to Kansas, investigated the election, found it fraudulent and over turned it.

The first two skirmishes had happened with no clear result or advantage for either side. In New England abolitionist sentiment was growing at a fever pitch. In Boston the abolitionist leader Henry Ward Beecher raised funds to send 1,200 armed abolitionists to Kansas. The 'Sharpe's rifles' as they were called arrived in Kansas in boxes labeled "Bibles." The stage was set for something far more serious then fund raising and fraudulent elections. Both sides stared at one another through prisms of hatred and thoughts of violence.

In October of 1855 an abolitionist from Pennsylvania arrived in Kansas. His name was John Brown.

Brown had spent time in abolitionist strongholds such as Boston and Philadelphia. He was enraged by the beating of Senator Sumner and was convinced that pro slave people were by nature unrefined and prone to violence. When he and his sons arrived in Kansas they were heavily armed and certain of rightness of their anti-slavery beliefs.

Soon Brown's strident rhetoric and growing reputation for violence had made him well known throughout the territory. In what is called the Pottawatomie Massacre he and his sons were said to have lured five pro slavers to a creek and hacked them to death with swords. Brown visited the new territorial legislature demanding violent attacks on border ruffians and their slave owning friends. Brown fought in at least two pitched batters, Palmyra and Osawatomie, while in the territory.

In October, 1856 Brown and his sons left Kansas and went north to raise funds, purchase weapons and recruit followers. Abolitionist speaking tours, rallies, marches and a brief return trip to Kansas marked these years. If most of the nation had forgotten about John Brown it was to be rudely reminded by his next move.

By 1859 Brown was convinced that an armed uprising by slaves against their property owning masters was the only answer. Having raised enough funds to buy thousands of medieval style pikes as well as modern fire arms Brown decided to use them by staging a raid on the federal arsenal in Harper's Ferry, Virginia. He was convinced that once weapons had been made available slaves by the thousands would flock to his ranks. Brown was better at fund raising that recruiting. In early October he arrived in Harper's Ferry to await his volunteers. In the end it was John Brown and eighteen others.

Nothing frightened and alarmed the southern states like the prospect of slave rebellion. A recurring theme of southern politics was the brutal uprising of slaves and the massacre and rape of the white population. Slaves had fought with Britain during the revolutionary war in hopes that a British victory would mean the end of slavery and their freedom. During the War of 1812 the British encouraged slaves to flee and in thousands of small incursions along the southern coast many did. At wars end Britain relocated 12,000 runaway slaves to the underpopulated island of Bermuda while refusing southern demands that their property be returned.

In 1831 a slave named Nat Turner had famously led a rebellion in Virginia. Armed only with farm tools he and his followers killed about sixty slave owners all the while gathering weapons, more escaped slaves and confidence. The terrified Virginians called out their militias and unable to find Turner turned their wrath on other slaves killing up to 200 of them for no reason other than their status. The actual rebellion was suppressed rather quickly but Turner escaped and hid in the woods for several months. Eventually captured he was hanged November 11, 1831 and the slave owners had his body flayed, drawn and quartered and burned for good measure. (Taylor, Alan. *"The Internal Enemy: Slavery and War in Virginia 1772-1832."* Norton, (2013).

In the aftermath of political compromise, Sumner's beating and what was by now called "Bloody Kansas" the south could not have been more worried about being killed by their slaves. By choosing to attempt a slave rebellion, particularly one in which the slaves had modern weapons, Brown could not have struck a more terrifying chord. One guaranteed to provoke the wrath and hatred among the slave owning southerners.

Brown waited until October 16 to launch his rebellion. Finally convinced that no additional reinforcements were coming his men seized the arsenal in the early morning hours. At first things went smoothly but soon the unexpected arrival of a quite innocent train sparked shooting that left a railroad worker and four of Brown's men dead.

Local citizens sounded the alarm and quickly formed militias that forced Brown and his followers inside the brick arsenal where they were besieged. The rebels had attempted to cut all telegraph lines but had been attacked by the locals before finishing the job. Within hours the military in Baltimore was alerted. The rebellion had failed. But it was not yet over.

On October 18 a battalion of US Marines, prophetically commanded by Robert E. Lee, arrived in Harper's Ferry. Brown was given the opportunity to surrender and refused. Lee than ordered an assault. It took the Marines about three minutes to knock down the doors and kill or capture the defenders. Among those who survived was an injured by defiant John Brown.

That Brown had committed serious crimes was evident. But given the times the central question was whether those crimes were federal or state. The decision was important since a federal prosecution would mean transport to Philadelphia or Baltimore where the jury would be composed of local citizens. If the prosecution was in state court it would mean that the jury would be made up of the outraged citizens of Harper's Ferry.

In a time when both sides seemed committed to the most provocative acts possible Virginia claimed jurisdiction and held a hasty trial in Harper's Ferry. On November 2 Brown was found guilty of sedition and murder by a state court jury. He was sentenced to death.

On December 2, 1959 a large crowd gathered in Harper's Ferry to witness Brown's execution. The south was convinced that an armed rescue attempt would be made and the military was out in force. Once again commanded by Robert E. Lee who in addition to being of the highest ranking officers in the US Army was a Lieutenant Colonel in the Virginia militia. Lee had with him some soon to be famous men.

J.E.B. Stuart had personally delivered the surrender demand to the men trapped in the arsenal. Cadets from Virginia Military Academy were commanded by a captain named Thomas R. Jackson. In less than two years he would be known as "Stonewall."

The crowd hushed as Brown mounted the scaffold. He had refused a blindfold and although still suffering from his wounds was as defiant as ever. He was asked if he had any last words. He did and they rang prophetically as they placed the noose around his neck.

"The crimes of this guilty land," he said, "can be expiated only in blood." (Reynolds, David S., *"John Brown Abolitionist; the man who killed slavery, sparked the civil war and seeded civil rights"*, Knopf, (2005).

To the south John Brown became everything hated. A self-righteous northerner determined to both judge and change them. A fanatic sent by the devil to destroy their way of life. Photos and drawings of him were circulated in every state. In them he looked deranged rather like some old testament Abraham gone returned to do the devil's work. His image became synonymous with everything hateful about "Yankees."

But in the north Brown became an instant hero. More than that he became a martyr to the abolitionist cause. The fact that this noble man had been tried by a Virginia jury was proof of his martyrdom. Denied justice by a racist slave owning southern jury (none of the jurors actually owned slaves) he had been denied a fair trial. "John Brown's Body" became the anthem of the anti-slavery movement. Contrary to their use in the south his image was carried at the fore of abolitionist marches and rallies that now spread out of New England into all the northern states.

For practical purposes the execution of John Brown was the moment where the quarreling elements of US society could no longer find common ground. No one tried. The United States of America, so carefully created by the delegates to the constitutional convention some eighty years before, simply came apart at the seams.

The compromises required to achieve union in the first place were simply not sustainable. The constitutional delegates had attempted to limit federal power by stating that states would retain powers not specifically granted the federal government. That was and is open to interpretation and thus the constant conflict between federal power and state rights. When it developed that political power in Congress depended on a balance of membership between states that embraced slavery and those that abhorred it the essential element of union became either more compromise or, if neither side could obtain a decisive political power (something neither side was willing to concede the other) rupture.

For whatever reasons rupture was what occurred.

To appreciate that we must remember that both sides felt so strongly about this issue that they were willing to walk away from politics and talk and dissolve the very union they both purported to love.

The federal v state rub over power is fundamental to the country's very existence. Nothing is more deeply ingrained and nothing makes people more angry and confrontational. Today the refusal of some states to allow Medicaid expansion is the perfect modern example of this age old tension. On balance, they reason, it is better to sentence people with disabilities to an early death than it is to accept money from Washington, DC.

This basic tenet of United States life leaves people with disabilities forever wondering who to turn to for recognition, support and welcoming. Is it a powerful central government in Washington, DC that can both create and enforce equal rights, opportunities and protection or are those things better delivered by states with no federal interference? Twenty five years ago when Congress was debating the Americans with Disabilities Act a strong argument against was a fear of federal power. This tension has been present from the first and has never gone away. There have been times where it appeared one side or the other had won. But with the passage of an election or two it returns.

But for people with disabilities the most chilling part of the *Dred Scott* decision was its ruling that no one other than white people (specifically white male people) enjoyed any legal rights whatsoever. Millions of living humans were officially nonexistent. The country was not for them. Returning to the three fifths compromise the failure to directly deal with the issue of slavery meant that a decision was simply delayed. As we have seen it would not go away and could not be delayed forever. Ultimately the union came apart over its official fiction that slaves simply didn't legally exist.

This raises the question of how long a modern democracy can endure without recognizing and reacting to the just claims of all of its' people? Today everyone is allegedly welcome but in practice we all know that millions of people in dozens of categories are systematically discriminated against every day. High on that list are people with disabilities.

The pre-civil war United States came undone because of exclusion. Or, put another way, by failure to include. Is inclusion then simply a goal for a society or is it an essential element required for long term survival? Are we ignoring the needs of citizens at our own risk? How long can oppression last before the politics of confrontation arises? This interplay of who is in, who is out and who decides is with us today as much as in the past. Thinking about these commonalities across generations may not lead us to immediate answers. But it certainly allows us to think seriously about them. And that alone is a good first step.

THE NATION IN TATTERS—CIVIL WAR.

The Harper's Ferry raid and subsequent execution of John Brown destroyed all but the thinnest pretext of union. Both sides now eyed one another with suspicion, paranoia and a growing regional hatred. The US Civil

War may not have started as a war to *free* the slaves but it was most certainly fought *because* of them. Eighty years earlier delegates to the constitutional convention forged a new nation by compromising on the issue of slavery. That compromise now came home to roost with a vengeance. However altruistic the founders may or may not have been their experiment came apart in 1861. It turned out that a nation founded for the benefit of white male property owners had a fatal flaw. And that flaw was the systematic exclusion of millions of people.

In November, 1860 Abraham Lincoln was elected President of the United States. Although Lincoln had at no time in his career called for the abolition of slavery the southern states suspected him of abolitionist sentiment and reacted accordingly.

Lincoln was inaugurated on March 4, 1861. Before he had drawn a breath as the new president southern states had begun to leave the union. The first was South Carolina who left in December, 1860. Mississippi, Florida and Alabama left in January of 1861. The Union was broken over the issue of state rights and slavery before Lincoln could take office.

During the weeks following his inauguration Lincoln and others looked on rather hopelessly attempting to find yet another compromise to keep the country together. The south was not having it. The succeeding states met in March, 1861 to form a new nation called the Confederate States of America and declared their independence. On April 12, 1861 the South Carolina militia opened fire on Fort Sumter in the harbor of Charleston. With the outbreak of hostility Georgia, Louisiana, Virginia and Texas quickly left the union. The most murderous war in US history had begun.

The US civil war would last until April 9, 1865 when confederate General Robert E. Lee surrendered the

Army of Northern Virginia at Appomattox courthouse. The war has been called the first modern one. And indeed it was. For one thing the theater of operations was huge. Military campaigns stretched from the Texas border to Maryland and from the Ohio River all the way to the Gulf of Mexico. There were even skirmishes in the territories and in faraway California.

The south went to war with little understanding of the industrial nature of modern warfare. As the years bled by the industrial might of the northern states played a larger and larger role. The war marked the first in which railroads played a decisive role and the north had hundreds of times the miles of primitive track in the south. The term 'scorched earth' first entered the lexicon of warfare in both the Shenandoah Valley of Virginia and in the states of Georgia and South Carolina. By war's end the south was defeated in every way imaginable. Infrastructure was destroyed, the economy in ruins and the population uprooted. Most important the south had lost its slaves.

That the war was murderous is well known. Estimates of combat and disease deaths vary. The most common figure cited in 620,000. (Fox and Livermore, 1889) More recent studies put the death toll at up to 850,000. (Hacker, David. J. University of Birmingham, 2012).

There are a number of ways to contemplate those numbers. That they are by far the highest in US history, including two World Wars, is clear. To feel the emotional impact on the nation it is instructive to compare those numbers to US deaths in World War II.

In 1860 the population of the US was 31.5 million. In 1945 the population of the US was 140 million. Total US deaths in the Second World War total 407,000. Allowing for changes in population had that war been fought at the lethal severity of the Civil War US combat deaths would have been about 2,752,800.

Slightly over 2 million soldiers fought in the war. More than one in three lost their life. The country had never imagined anything like it. When peace came in the spring of 1865 both sides were disgusted, worn out and desperate to do anything else. For both sides peace could not have come soon enough. (See also Grant, Ulysses S, *"Memoirs and Selected Letters"* The Library of America (1990).

POLITICAL REACTION—THE "CIVIL WAR" AMENDMENTS.

Congress, which of course was made up only of delegates from the victorious northern states, moved to insure the south was both punished and rendered subordinate to the federal power in Washington, DC.

In 1865 the thirteenth amendment to the Constitution was adopted. Slavery was abolished. With one act of Congress and ratification by the states the most contentious issue ever was resolved. Slavery was dead.

Three years later congress adopted the fourteenth amendment. Of the amendments this one is by far the most important. Although its promise would lay dormant for a century it is this amendment which would eventually be the lynchpin of legal arguments that not only broke the back of segregation but also is the basis for victories by a fledgling new force; the Disability Rights Movement. The text of Article I (quoted below) is the legal foundation for advances not only by former slaves but eventually by women and people with disabilities. This language resonates to this day.

"No state shall make or enforce any law which shall abridge the privileges and immunities of citizens of the United States, nor shall any state deprive any person of life, liberty or property without due process of law; not deny to any person within its jurisdiction the equal protection of the law."

The fifteenth amendment followed in 1870. It declared it unlawful to deny a citizen the right to vote based on 'race, color, or previous condition of servitude.'

Slavery was abolished. All were guaranteed due process of law. Former slaves could vote and federal power would guarantee it all. The country set out with new principles of governance. Principles it hoped would lead to more fairness, equality and opportunity for all. It was to be a golden age of equality and inclusion.

That dream lasted until the great political betrayal of 1876.

AMBITION, BETRAYAL, APARTHEID: THE COMPROMISE OF 1877.

The end of the civil war left the nation worn out physically, economically and spiritually. The ravaged former slave states in particular longed for their lost, and mostly imaginary, antebellum glory. Both sides longed for their boys who went to war. About half of all war deaths in United States history had just happened to a nation a fraction of the size that it would become. And there were the disabled.

The number of disabled veterans who came home from war is not known. Estimates range widely but it was in the millions. The country was still agrarian. A land of small farms and family operations. To sustain that way of life meant that boys and young men must work very hard. There was land to clear, crops to grow, fences to build, animals to husband, children to raise and the old folks to bury. But in many parts of the country those boys and young men were either dead or disabled. For many it was simply impossible to continue life patterns that had taken generations to form. Thousands of survivors simply gave up, joined with who they could, and moved west. They left behind abandoned homestead, untilled fields and a sense of emptiness, under population and for the south a palpable sense of loss and grief.

All those who had borne arms in the confederate army were barred from voting until they took very public loyalty oaths to the hated northern government. The process was inefficient, slow and to many former southern soldiers insulting and intentionally humiliating. Thousands simply refused to make what they considered a plea for forgiveness when in their eyes they had done nothing but their duty. The number of white voters in the former slave states dropped. And for the first time, with the muscle of the federal army of occupation at hand, former slaves-now-citizens voted. They voted by the tens of thousands and quickly obtained political power unimaginable a few years before. To white southerners this was far from a reason to rejoice. Many saw their beloved culture as being destroyed by racially inferior former slaves. Fear of reprisals was as acute as the old fear of slave rebellion. Just below the surface hatred seethed. In December of 1865 in Pulaski, Tennessee an organization was formed that took the name Ku Klux Klan. Their purpose was simple. To turn back the clock by the use of violence against the former slaves. (See Foner, Eric. *Reconstruction: America's Unfinished Revolution, 1863-1877,* Perennial Classics, (1988))

Despite white resentment former slaves were adjusting to a life of freedom. Between 1866 and 1877 more than two thousand former slaves were elected to and held public office. That list included two United States senators from Mississippi. Seven United States representatives from the states of Virginia, Mississippi, South Carolina, Alabama and Florida. Hundreds of lesser offices such as county judges, clerks, assessors and sheriffs were also filled with former slaves. Majorities were reached in state legislatures and all of this happened in spite of the growing size and violence of the Klan. (Foner, Eric (Ed) *"Freedom's Lawmakers: A Directory of Black Office Holders during Reconstruction."* Louisiana State University press, (1996).

The former slaves of the south had been guaranteed full citizenship by the recent constitutional amendments and the northern army remained behind to enforce those rights as necessary. The army acted as an army of occupation with the power of martial law, armed action and aggressive law enforcement. The embittered south may have a few successful night raids and lynching by the Klan but they were no match for the discipline and fire power of the army. Pitched battles were sometimes fought. Southern men were caught, hanged or jailed. Only one thing kept the former slaves from being violently persecuted and that was the military might of the army. An indignity the south found harder and harder to bear.

Here is a good place to reflect on just what all this means for Americans with intellectual and developmental disabilities at the beginning of a new century. Politics, then and now, is the authoritative allocation of advantages and disadvantages between and among the people. How that process plays out in the United States in terms of who is in and who is out follows to this day the same swings in mood as those we have been tracking from the constitutional convention. As we shall soon see more is known about the thousands of Afro-Americans lynched in the south than is known of the perhaps hundreds of thousands of Americans with intellectual and developmental disabilities who perished in institutions during the same time.

The first of these of course is the strength of a powerful federal government able to exert its authority over the states and compel uniform administration of justice against power lying with the individual states. Each of which can decide for themselves how things are to be. Back and forth these pendulums swing. Adams lost his election because Jefferson accused him of abusing his power. After winning Jefferson continued the same policies and bought the Louisiana Territory to boot. States insisted on their rights to bring slavery into new lands. A strong federal government could stop that. Tension over that issue repeated itself over and over in the compromises made to keep the country together. From the perspective of a disability advocate the post-civil war federal power seems pretty attractive since it guaranteed enforcement of the new civil rights laws. To the state rights people of their day federal power did not mean liberty. It meant tyranny by a far off evil power in Washington telling them what to do.

The Affordable Care Act (ACA), also known as Obamacare, is a perfect contemporary example of these same patterns. Access to affordable health care and particularly the end of the hated pre-existing condition exemption which allowed insurance companies to charge high prices or deny coverage at their whim, has for generations been one of our priorities. The ACA, while not perfect, offers for the first time some meaningful reforms that people with disabilities badly need and want.

Community living and self-directed lives are key to inclusion. A provision of the ACA, known as the Community First Choice Option, can create a federal and state partnership to fund the costs of personal attendants, transportation, housing and other things that are barriers to independent living. However, it requires state legislatures and governors to adopt it. Adoption means the influx of millions of federal dollars. Rejection means people live solely on the whim of local politicians.

Seldom go we see a clearer example of the great divide over federal power. The greatness of the divide can be appreciated here because the feared encroachment of state rights is merely money. Accept the money and advantages in your state can be authoritatively allocated to the advantage of people with disabilities who wish to live in the community. Rejection means advantages can be authoritatively allocated in favor of anti-Washington politics, for profit nursing homes, institutions, etc.

One would think that choice easy. But in fact 'red' states, including those of the old confederacy, have mostly rejected the expansion of Medicaid services. Why? Because the nearly mystical attraction of local control is more important and powerful than the needs of disabled citizens. The fight over federalism continues just as it did in 1804. The same conflicts are still with us. And in their intensity over this issue policy makers very simply disregard large groups of people who are a sort of collateral damage to the bigger philosophical issue.

Which brings us to the second issue we have been tracking. The ability of the powerful to simply become blind to millions of people who do not neatly fit in their perspective of who matters, who belongs and who is included. The three fifths compromise got the country off on a false start by pretending that millions of humans simply did not exist. Or, if they did, they were not important.

The conflict over state rights and who belongs is much with us. It is pretty easy to overlook the suffering of people with disabilities who long to be free when you come from a political tradition based on ignoring people needs to achieve some 'higher' goal. We have not yet even touched on manifest destiny and the extermination of Native American peoples. But for a political tradition that innocently asks 'where did all the Indians go?' ignoring a few million people with disabilities is easy.

We have seen how white male property owners joined together to form a nation for themselves. Profits, property, control, prestige and entitlement of the elites have been from the beginning the most powerful decision maker in politics. When a formerly ignored minority begins to assert itself (as the former slaves did and people with disabilities are) these powerful forces can come together and make some self-serving deals that shock the world by their hypocrisy.

THE ELECTION OF 1876—APARTHEID COMES TO THE SOUTH.

There are moments and events that illustrate that truth. The election of 1876 is perhaps the most obvious. Not only were the elites able to meet in secret and reach a deal that disenfranchised Afro-Americans in the south for a century but they were able to make it seem so legitimate and normal that today hardly anyone remembers what really happened, why, and its consequences. And, my friends, if they can do it to millions of people they allegedly just fought a war to free they can do to people with disabilities without breaking a sweat.

The constitutional convention had been heavily influenced by the revolution in France. Many of the delegates regarded themselves as a part of the French enlightenment and greatly admired the work of Rousseau,

Voltaire, Diderot and others. The lofty language coming from France provided much of the verbiage. But the Paris mob also made an impression on the delegates. Unfettered democracy smacked to them as an invitation to mob rule. Distrustful of the popular vote they insulated the office of President of the United States by establishing the Electoral College. It is the vote of that college that actually confers power on the winner. And that college is in no way bound to cast their votes consistent with the popular vote. For selfish political reasons the election of 1876 showed this flaw and how easy it is to steal an election if the right power people desire it. Here is the sordid story.

The now martyred Abraham Lincoln was succeeded in 1865 by his vice president Andrew Johnson of Tennessee. His sad term sort of petered out and in 1868 war hero and savior of the nation, General of the Army Ulysses S. Grant was elected president. He was elected to a second term in 1872. In spite of the scandals and allegations of corruption Grant remained personally popular and it was widely expected that he would seek a third term in 1876. However, with the sudden death of his vice president Grant announced his retirement from politics. With him out to the picture a mad scramble followed.

Both major parties smelled opportunity. And so did some minor ones. It was clear that a new era was about to dawn. Who would lead it?

It is important to remember that the political parties of mid-19th century politics were far different from what they now are. The republicans were the liberals. The Party of Lincoln saw itself as the liberator of the slaves. They favored a strong central government in order to control the former treasonous south. In our come-and-go dance of federalism vs state rights the republicans were the federalists.

The democrats were the conservatives. During the bitter debate on reconstruction that marked the administration of President Johnson they favored a conciliatory approach to the south and were generally nervous about the freed slaves and what they feared were radical changes in the regional power blocks.

Both parties convened conventions during the summer of 1876. Neither party had a clear favorite.

The sixth republican national convention was held in Cincinnati, Ohio and after seven highly charged ballots the delegates chose the 'favorite son' candidate and Governor of Ohio Rutherford B. Hayes.

A few weeks later the 12th Democratic Party convention was held in St. Louis. Like the republicans the delegates deadlocked through several ballots before nominating New York Governor Samuel J. Tilden.

In addition three minor parties were also on the ballot. The Greenback Party that favored the issuing of more paper money. The Prohibition Party whose ambitions would finally bear fruit in 1920 with the adoption of the 21st amendment forbidding alcoholic beverages. Finally the American Nation Party whose platform, ironically, was abolition of the Electoral College.

When the election was over Tilden had won an absolute majority of all votes cast. A total of 50.9% Hayes was second with 47.9%. In terms of the crucial Electoral College votes Tilden had won 184 to Hayes 165. Twenty electoral votes were disputed.

Competing factions in Florida, Louisiana and South Carolina simply each reported that their man had won. In far off Oregon an elector was found to have been fraudulently chosen and had to be replaced.

An 'electoral commission' was formed to decide what to do. In fact it was what was by now called 'bosses' who met in secret and hashed out a deal that would forever change the United States. Once again the principles of life, liberty and pursuit of happiness were set aside by the white male property owning elite that actually ran things. In the end and spite of the popular vote Rutherford B. Hayes was awarded all twenty of the disputed votes and was declared the winner. (Rehnquist, William. *"Centennial Crisis: the Disputed Election of 1876"*. Vintage Books. 2005).

In exchange for the democrats not challenging the election the republicans agreed to Hayes' election and with it the removal of all federal forces from the south. The army of occupation left in the spring of 1877 and with it the federal power to protect the former slaves and assure that the Civil War amendments were enforced. Once again, to avoid conflict with their own elite partners, a compromise was reached. Democrats got what they wanted and republicans were able to wash their hands of whole racial mess.

In the span of a mere twelve years the federal power vs state power pendulum had swung from one extreme to the other. In 1865 it appeared that the issue had once and for all been laid to rest by the union victory. By 1876 federal power virtually disappeared from the old south. All decisions, such as voting, property ownership, public places, schools etc. were to be left to the states. The north was aware of the "Negro" problem but was satisfied to leave it to their southern countrymen, who after all, 'knew best' how to solve it. Or at least to keep it quiet. Or at least to relieve themselves of any sense of responsibility for the millions of people whose lives had just been put in the hands of vengeful former slave owners and their bitter allies. (Morris, Roy Jr. *"Fraud of the Century: Rutherford B. Hayes, Samuel Tilden, and the Stolen Election of 1876*", Simon and Schuster, 2004.) What happened is well described in a recent report by the Congressional Research Office.

"Federal troops were withdrawn from the south and the political gains of the 'freed men' were rolled back. Most blacks were prevented from voting by tactics such as literacy tests, poll taxes as well as intimidation and violence. By the turn of the 20th Century blacks were completely disenfranchised in the south." Coleman, Kevin J. March 10, 2015.

With the shake of a hand and the wink of an eye all the changes promised by the Civil War vanished. The south returned to a political economy resembling its pre-war condition. A condition that denied any legal protections whatsoever to the former slaves.

Apartheid descended over the south that would last nearly a century. Black people were reduced to second class citizens if they were lucky. Without the protection of any law enforcement they found themselves imprisoned in a system that denied their humanity, forced poverty on them and then blamed them for being poor, raped women, hung men, kept the children illiterate and disgraced every principle of the very constitution the segregationist pointed to for justification of their "state rights."

The North looked the other way.

Make no mistake the Jim Crow south was much more than just separate. It was held together by violence which could be unleashed at any time for any reason. Using a white only facility, a head not properly bowed, smiling at the wrong time, any sign of ambition in the white world was likely to be met with violence. Not just beatings but death.

A lot of scholarship has gone into finding an answer to the question 'how many people were lynched during Jim Crow'? No one will ever know for certain. Certainly hundreds and more likely thousands were hung from trees or burnt alive in the dead of night. Their bodies never found, identified or accounted for. By now the Klan included judges, police, officials' of all kinds, clergy, farmers, teachers and seemingly anyone.

Recently the Equal Justice Initiative in Atlanta identified 3,959 named victims of 'racial terror lynching." That grim number began in 1877 and ended in 1950. Not a single white person was ever prosecuted for murdering a black one. Well and truly a reign of terror that far eclipsed the more famous one in Paris. No data is available on the number of rapes and beatings beyond knowing that they were common place. If ever there has been a governing system based on terror it was the Jim Crow South of the United States of America.

Murder is a crime that, by destroying individual lives, violates the legal and moral order of the community; extermination is a crime that, by destroying an entire community is a crime against the family of communities that make up mankind—a crime, as international law has come to realize "against humanity." Murder is a crime against the living; extermination is a crime against the future. This is what the philosopher Hannah Arendt calls "the banality of evil." Terror, segregation, servitude were so ordinary as to be invisible. It was just the 'way things are.' Indeed it is that sense of normalcy that had been the essential props of the gigantic, insane, state-sponsored crimes of our time. Or, put another way, there are none as blind as they who will not see.

When the state becomes an exterminator of human spirit as well as life, and the law, instead of enjoining evil, supports and enforces it—as does the whole tremendous weight of custom, habit, bureaucratic inertia, and social pressure—the individual who might seek to oppose the policies is left in an extremity of moral solitude. To expect individuals, alone and unsupported, to resist official dictate is to expect a lot.

Emanuel Kant identified radical evil (as opposed to ordinary evil) as that which occurs when the will, even when unafraid or unswayed by temptation, somehow inspires itself to commit evil. No passion or personal animosity is required to simply follow instructions and fill the role of functionary in a system which makes a commodity of suffering and dependency. The human beings whose lives and those of their children, grandchildren and great-grandchildren were destroyed by the Compromise of 1877 were all victims of radical evil.

It was not necessary for the white elites who agreed to this 'compromise' to hate or even dislike the former slaves. The needs and aspirations of black people in the south were so unimportant as to not be a factor in the decision. They were simply in the way. Once again that trait of pretending groups of people do not exist reared its head.

This is a good place for the disability rights movement to ponder this phenomena. As we point to and celebrate successes over the past half century it is essential to know that they can vanish in an afternoon. All we have to do is get ourselves between the 'big boys' and their ambitions and suddenly we could find ourselves as invisible, powerless and expendable as the former slaves.

No act happens in a moral vacuum. The fact that history may be a harsh judge does nothing to prevent deeds rooted in radical evil from happening now. It does not make us weak to know that we are vulnerable to whims of the moment. Knowledge (I do believe) is power and the more we appreciate how power works the safer we will be.

This waxing and waning of fortune in American history is not just something that happened to Native Americans and Afro-Americans. All they did was get in the way of a larger agenda. That made them expendable. Money is power and power is money and it is the task of our movement to make sure we have plenty of both. Otherwise we are simply dabbling on the edge of a political world we can flirt with but not command. A lesson to remember.

1877-1965 APARTHEID COMES TO THE UNITED STATES OF AMERICA.

Apartheid, according to Webster's Dictionary, is 'a rigid policy of segregation of the non-white population.' Although the word is most commonly used to describe South Africa it is difficult to distinguish any meaningful difference from the condition of 'free' Afro-Americans living in the former confederate states. Apartheid or not the southern system of racial segregation was enforced as rigidly as anything in South Africa and was supported by terror. Far from being some lost 'golden age' of state rights it was a time of disgrace that will blight the nation forever.

Prior to the Compromise of 1877, and the removal of federal troops from the south, about half a million former slaves registered to vote. (Constitutional Rights Foundation). To most of the freed slaves President Abraham Lincoln was their 'great emancipator' and, accordingly, they predominately voted for the Republican Party. As the political pendulum swung between state rights and federal power federalism reached its 19th

Century apex with Lee's surrender at Appomattox. To a naïve or untrained eye this block of solidly 'liberal' voters assured the continued supremacy of radical republican reconstruction policy. That could not have been more wrong. (See Stampp, Kenneth, *The Era of Reconstruction: 1865-1877,* Vintage Classics, (1967)).

We have seen repeatedly that the white male property owning men who created the country bequeathed to their sons a sense of entitlement and privilege that included whatever extrajudicial mischief was necessary protect their hegemony over the nation's real decision making. Once again they agreed on their desires. The north saved money on the army and was able to wash its' hands of the 'negro' problem while the south saw the fortunes of war dramatically turned in their favor. All it took was a handshake, a wink and an Electoral College fraud. The former slaves, ever excluded from the corridors of real power, were left on the sidelines to watch and await their fate. As human beings with rights, aspirations and dreams they counted for nothing in the great game of power.

What happened to the former slaves can happen to any group seen as in the way of the shifting desires of the real power brokers. In United States politics nothing is safe and nothing is forever.

When President Hayes ordered the army to withdraw from the south it took with it any shred of authority the federal government had to enforce the 13th, 14th and 15th amendments. All of that was the responsibility of the states and it did not take long for white supremacists to reclaim what they saw as theirs. Black voting dropped off everywhere as a result of threats from employers and the ever present menace of the Klan more bent than ever to establish white supremacy whatever the cost. Lynching and terror reigned.

As the new white majority began to vote out the black office holders they began to enact their own legislation designed to assure that political power would forever be denied their black neighbors.

If the republican party of the day was the one favoring civil and constitutional rights for the former slaves than the white voters needed a party of their own. The democrats were the conservative party of the day. Democrats favored states making the choices about things like voting rights. The south adopted the Democratic Party as their own and the 'solid south' voted democratic in every election until 1968 when Richard Nixon's 'southern strategy' adopted enough racist buzz words to appeal to them. The democrats, seen as the party of Lyndon Johnson and the Voting Rights Act was abandoned. The labels of liberal and conservative (for all of their shortcomings) were suddenly reversed. But that was far in the future when the former slaves faced knowing that their hopes and dreams of freedom had been sacrificed by some distant and mysterious process. Whatever that process was it did not care about them. That much was certain.

The 15th Amendment provided particularly challenging obstacles for the white supremacists. The amendment specifically forbade denying the vote to any citizen because of their race, color or previous condition of servitude. The amendment made it clear that they could not just outlaw voting by race. That would be unconstitutional. What they could do is pass laws making black voting impossible and they could do so comfortable in their knowledge that the federal government would do nothing to interfere with their 'local control.'

All of the former slave states used slightly different methods of suppressing votes by former slaves and later their descendants. Mississippi is a good example and in many ways was the most successful. Knowing that blacks were now marginalized and represented the poorest residents of the state their constitution of 1890 required voters to pay a semi-annual poll tax. It had to be paid two years in advance of the election the voter wished to participate in. This was an impossible economic burden for black Mississippians'. Most simply could not pay it.

Another common legislated barrier was the literacy test. On paper these sound innocuous enough. A potential voter was required to show up in person at the office of their county clerk. For many rural blacks that meant travelling to a white supremacy town where the risk of violence was ever present. Once there they were required to read portions of the state constitution out loud to the clerk and then explain what it meant. The clerk was always white and knew his job. His job was to decide that black voters were simply too illiterate to vote. Soon potential black voters simply gave up.

Evidence supporting the Voting Right Act would later include testimony that black men were asked to read and explain the most complicated parts of the constitution while whites were allowed to read the simplest. The county clerks turned down the vast majority of those attempting to register. (See Blockmon, Douglas A., *A Slavery by Another Name: The Re-enslavement of Black Americans from the Civil War to WW II,* Doubleday, (2008)).

Throughout the south states employed many strategies to eliminate the threat of Black voters. In Florida only property owners could vote. It didn't go quite as far as white male property owners but the values of the founders echoed in the ears of the racists who devised it.

Another strategy was the all-white primary. Blacks of course were free to vote in the general election. If they could register. These electoral schemes placed the top two vote getters from the primary election on the ballot without regard to party affiliation. Since the white majority voted solidly for the segregationist southern Democrats two of them were always the candidates. Registered Blacks were 'free' to vote for whichever Jim Crow candidate they liked. There was no republican (liberal) option available.

One of the most sinister methods of denying franchise to Black voters was the grandfather clause. To register you had to show that you or a direct relative had been registered to vote in elections held before 1863. Conveniently a few years before adoption of the 15th Amendment. Since 100% of southern voters at that time were white this gem succeeded in blocking any political participation by the former slaves.

I want to emphasize, particularly to people with disabilities who may feel safe under our current scheme of things, that all of the disenfranchisement and debasing of blacks in the south was completely legal. Acting under color of law the segregationist legislatures passed their laws, destroyed lives, pretended to be following the letter of the constitution and felt good about it. Not unlike the austerity budget legislative sessions currently causing people to lose their homes and independence and end up in for profit nursing homes. All perfectly nice. All perfectly legal. All serving the interests of the spiritual heirs of the white male property owners who created a government to protect themselves.

As the spiral of federal power versus state rights veered sharply toward a weak federal government there was simply no authority capable of protecting the constitutional rights of those deemed unworthy. No legal recourse was available. As Pompey the Great once said, "Don't quote laws to us. We carry swords." (Levy, *The Civil War*. Penguin. 1995).

Violence, intimidation and legalized segregation denied African Americans the power of the ballot. By the 20th Century they did not hold elected office. Black citizens had no say in what laws would be passed, how tax dollars would be spent or who their local officials would be. By 1940 3 percent of voting-age black men and women in the old confederacy were registered to vote. In Mississippi the number was less than 1 percent. (Constitutional Rights Foundation).

With federal power at its' lowest ebb the rest of the nation simply turned its back on the south. For the Democratic Party its "Dixiecrat" members of Congress could be counted on for international relations, some tax issues, prohibition, etc. The southern states were expected to deal with their own 'negro problem.' Just how they did that was not the concern of the rest of the country.

In every corner of the old south the lot of African American citizens was the same. No rights before the law. Daily humiliations involving public accommodations of all kinds. Separate schools. Separate drinking fountains. Separate colleges and universities. Jail for interracial marriage. Over it all hung the very real face of violence. Lynching, beatings, rape, economic deprivations, retaliatory evictions and grinding unemployment and poverty marked every city, town and hamlet. Absent national political concern it appeared that the Jim Crow south was here to stay.

On December 7, 1941 the Empire of Japan attacked the United States Pacific Fleet at its moorage in Pearl Harbor in the territory of Hawaii. A few days later Hitler's Germany declared war on the United States. The war had been raging for some time and was at the height of its ferocity. Over fifty million people perished worldwide. In May of 1945 Germany surrendered unconditionally to the Allied Powers.

In August the United States became (and still is) the first country to use nuclear weapons. A few days later the Empire of Japan surrendered as well.

A total of 12,209,236 United States military personnel participated in the war. (The National World War II Museum, New Orleans). Of that number 1.2 million were African-American. Although they came from all parts of the country the predominant number came from Southern states where their local communities did a good job of finding them and getting them to the selective service system. At first these soldiers were used exclusively for truck driving, maintenance and other support functions. But as those soldiers agitated for a more prominent role and casualty lists mounted eventually the military began to deploy them in combat rolls. At war's end 708 Afro-American soldiers had been killed. The remainder returned home to their hamlet places of birth. One of the strengths of apartheid was keeping people from seeing much of anything of the world outside of a southern county or two. That all changed at wars end.

Over a million soldiers returned to 'peace.' At war's end the military was as segregated and racist as any part of Mississippi. All of the soldiers had first-hand experiences with racism and humiliation and many of them had seen men and women die.

For nearly all of them the lingering question was why. Why should they fight and die for a country where they could not stay in a decent hotel or patronize a restaurant? Where they could be hung from a tree for merely glancing at a white woman or failing to tip a hat to a passing white? They had fought for democracy but could not vote in their own towns and cities. They had seen something of the world and it was a lot bigger than they had thought.

All over the south veterans began to think about what kind of world they would leave to their children. What about the sacrifices of their dead comrades?

Seeds of hope that had lain fallow for a century slowly began to sprout in the South and beyond. And not just among Afro-Americans.

On May 29, 1935 six young adults in New York City demanded to meet with the director of the federal agencies created during the depression to aid in economic development. Told that the director was out they vowed to wait 'until hell freezes over.' Next day they were backed by a much larger crowd of sympathetic demonstrators demanding to know where their economic relief would come from. What was different about these people was their militant attitude and the fact that all of them had physical disabilities. They called themselves The League of the Physically Handicapped. The modern disability rights movement was born. (Longmore, Paul. *Why I Burned My Book and Other Essays on Disability.* Temple University Press (2003)).

The United States, whether it realized it or not, was about to experience a revolution of rising expectation unlike anything it had ever experienced before. Change was still to come. But it was stirring.

THE RETURN OF FEDERAL POWER: *BROWN VS. THE BOARD OF EDUCATION.*

The return of Afro-American veterans contributed greatly to an as yet unformed and unfocused sense of longing and a questioning of just why their lives were destined from birth to be ones of poverty and exploitation. As a sign that times were starting to change President Harry Truman signed an Executive Order in July, 1948 directing that all branches of the armed forces integrate immediately. (James, Rawn, Jr. *The Double V: How War, Protest and Harry Truman Desegregated America's Military.* Bloomsbury (2013)).

For the first time there was also an emerging middle class of educated Afro-Americans beginning to take shape in the northern states. These young men and women had tasted freedom and were wondering why it had been denied to so many for so long. They also wondered what they could do about it. The Civil Rights Movement was still in the future but its kernels were beginning to sprout in the minds of many young people.

One of those young people was a Baltimore lawyer named Thurgood Marshall. Both his great-grandfather and his grandfather had been slaves. Marshall was born in Baltimore in 1908 to a family that was far from typical of the kinds the apartheid south would allow. Marshall's father William was a railroad porter. Today that may not seem like a lot but in those days railroad porters were organized into a powerful union founded by A. Philip Randolph, the Brotherhood of Sleeping Car Porters. Union membership guaranteed William Marshall not only a solid middle class income but also travel and interactions with other men of his generation.

Norma Marshall was Thurgood's mother. She was a college graduate and a teacher. Young Thurgood's childhood was far different in Baltimore than it would have been in Birmingham or any other southern city. His family believed strongly in the power of education as a tool of liberation and he grew up with stimulating dinner conversations and the expectation that he would go on to college. (King, Gilbert. *Devil in the Grove: Thurgood Marshall, the Groveland Boys and the Dawn of a New America.* Harper (2013)).

After high school graduation (a considerable feat for any young Afro-American man of his time) he enrolled in Liberty University in Oxford, Pennsylvania. Liberty was one of a number of historically black universities that had sprung up as answers to black education in the face of segregationist policies that kept them out of state and private colleges and universities. Liberty was the first of these to grant degrees.

By the 1920s the intellectual environment of Liberty was lively and stimulating as evidenced by the fact that two of Marshall's classmates were the musician Cab Calloway and the poet Langston Hughes. He remained friends with them both all of his life. He graduated in 1929 with degrees in both American Literature and Philosophy. For the young Thurgood Marshall the next stop was law school.

He had hoped to attend law school near his family home in Baltimore. The University of Maryland Law School was closed to him by its 'whites only' admission policy. Instead he enrolled in another traditionally black college, Howard University in the District of Columbia. In 1933 he graduated number one in his class. He returned home to Baltimore and opened a private practice.

In 1934 Marshall began taking cases from the National Association for the Advancement of Colored People (NAACP). A famous collaboration what would last more than three decades. To his great delight his first notable case was *Murray v. Patton* which prophetically forced the University of Maryland to integrate its law school. It was the first of many triumphs he was to enjoy. Between his time with the NAACP (of which he became General Counsel) and his much later time as Solicitor General he would argue 32 cases in the Supreme Court of the United States. He won 29. (Williams, Juan. *Thurgood Marshall: American Revolutionary.* Three Rivers Press (2013)).

The first mention of Topeka, Kansas is on a proposed route to the west in 1826. It is pleasantly located along the banks of the Kansas River in northeast Kansas near the very center of the United States. According to the city web site the word Topeka means "a good place to plant potatoes.' Kansas is a part of the Louisiana Purchase and played an important role (as we have seen) in the antislavery movement of the 1850s. In fact Topeka was the first city in Kansas to be officially founded as a result of the Compromise of 1854. It was created by antislavery men late in that year and was staunchly abolitionist throughout the civil war. In 1861 it became the state capital.

In 1950 approximately 80,000 people lived in Topeka. About ten thousand were Afro-American. Among them was a railroad welder named Oliver Brown. Brown was also assistant pastor at St. Mark's AME Church. His daughter walked six blocks to and from school each day at Monroe Elementary. (Now the Brown v Board of Education National Historic Site). The school was 100% segregated. That same year the NAACP targeted Kansas schools as possible litigation sites. Thirteen Afro-American parents eventually agreed to be plaintiffs in a law suit to integrate the schools. Oliver Brown was the only male and was named chief plaintiff. A move that was to make him a very famous man.

As part of the preparations all of the plaintiffs temporarily withdrew their children from Monroe and one by one attempted to register them in white only public schools. All of the children were denied admission. Although Brown and the others lost the subsequent trial based on those claims they did help to create a record that could be appealed.

Sometime in the summer of 1951 Mr. Oliver Brown, railroad worker from Topeka, Kansas met Mr. Thurgood Marshall, son of a railroad worker in Baltimore, Maryland. Together they were about to rock the foundations of the United States in a way they had not been rocked since the south fired on Fort Sumter some ninety years before.

THE CASE.

In 1952 Marshall, now chief counsel to the NAACP, successfully consolidated similar cases from the states of Delaware, South Carolina, Virginia and the District of Columbia. The Supreme Court of the United States agreed to hear them all as if they were one case. That one case still carried the name of Oliver Brown, mild mannered assistant pastor from Topeka, Kansas.

The case turned on two questions. One, was separate but equal legal and two, was the 14th Amendment ('no state shall...deny to any person...the equal protection of the laws.') violated if it was?

Once again on the eve of a crisis the same factors came to bear as the ones regarding the Louisiana Purchase and all of the rest. Who had power? The states or the federal government? If state laws requiring segregated education were unconstitutional did the 14th amendment give the federal court power to overturn them? This contentious discord has been present from the constitutional convention onwards. To understand US politics requires one to anticipate in which direction that pendulum of power is currently swinging.

Marshall's argument was complicated by the fact that in 1896, in the case of *Plessey v. Ferguson*, the court had already considered the same questions. In that case the court ruled that as long as the separate facilities for separate races were equal, the mere fact of segregation by race did not violate the 14th Amendment. It was Marshall's job to convince them to overrule a prior Supreme Court case. Something the court strongly dislikes doing.

On May 17, 1954 a unanimous Court, speaking through Mr. Chief Justice Earl Warren, ruled that separate but equal education was unconstitutional as a violation of the equal protection clause of the 14th Amendment. It was no longer required to discuss the question of 'equal' which had taken up so much attention at countless school board meetings and state legislatures. The only part that mattered was separate. Separate education was unconstitutional on its own. Furthermore the state laws that required segregated education were unconstitutional and struck down. (Patterson, James T. *Brown v. Board of Education: A Civil Rights Milestone.* Oxford (2002)).

For Oliver Brown the outcome brought satisfaction and considerable fame. He continued to live in Topeka. In 1961 he died of a heart attack in Missouri. His daughter helped to create the Brown Foundation for Educational Equity in 1988. He is remembered fondly by all who knew him. (Linder, Douglas. *The Brown v Board of Education of Topeka: An Account.* Retrieved 5 April 2015).

Thurgood Marshall became famous overnight. Loved by progressives and loathed by segregationists.

He raised the profile of the NAACP as well as contributing to a revolution of rising expectation among Afro-Americans and their allies nationwide.

In 1965 he was appointed Solicitor General of the United States. On September 1, 1967, after a stormy Senate confirmation hearing, he was sworn in as an Associate Justice of the Supreme Court. As the first Afro-American justice Marshall became one of the most beloved jurists in United States history. He served with distinction on the court until his death in January, 1993. (See Goldman, Roger. *Thurgood Marshall: Justice for All.* Carroll and Graf, (1993))

THE REACTION

For most legal scholars the biggest surprise of *Brown* was that the opinion was unanimous. It was obvious that the court wanted to revisit *Plessy v. Ferguson* and why else would they take review if not to replace that decision?

But to the states whose laws specifically required that schools be rigidly segregated by race the decision was received as if it were a surprise. Shock and anger resonated everywhere. To racially integrate their schools meant an end to a cherished tradition and a sense of local hegemony. That the veil of federal power had once again risen and under the guise of the 14th Amendment had destroyed a cherished cornerstone of their culture was nearly too much to bear. To say that the reaction was hysterical would not be too strong a descriptor.

KANSAS

The Topeka school board was the official loser in the decision. But Kansas moved rather quickly to comply. The school in question, Monroe Elementary, was a K-8 school. The high schools of Topeka had been integrated previously. In fact there had been discussion among Marshall and his colleagues as to whether or not Kansas was a good choice for the appeal. The test was thought to be separate but equal and Topeka schools were about as close to equal as could be imagined. As it turned out the only test was separate. Marshall's instincts had been right. (See Wilson, Paul A. *A Time to Lose: Representing Kansas in Brown vs. Board of Education.* University of Kansas Press (1995)).

FLORIDA

Within weeks of the decision the Florida legislature reacted by passing a resolution stating that all decisions of federal courts were 'null and void' within the states' borders. This novel approach was presented to the nation as the doctrine of interposition. Ever hopeful the states of Alabama and Mississippi passed similar resolutions. Their reaction was to simply state that they would ignore the federal power and continue life as normal. In Florida as well as the others a great deal of subsequent litigation followed as civil rights groups sued state governments for attempting various schemes at discrediting the decision and moving ahead as if it had not happened. The struggle to implement the decision in Florida dragged on for four decades. (Florida Advisory Commission to the US Commission on Civil Rights. Retrieved April 5, 2015).

NORTH CAROLINA

North Carolina adopted a strategy of tacitly accepting the decision but in tacitly resisting it in every way possible. Transition to a fully integrated school system did not begin until 1971 and then only because a series of successful local law suits as well as both violent and non-violent demonstrations.

VIRGINIA

Virginia promptly passed a law that there would no longer be attendance requirements for students at any integrated school. Warming to interposition they simply closed their schools while the issue was being 'studied.' In 1956 Governor Stanley recommended that no state funds be appropriated for any school that had integrated. That policy held until overturned by a federal court in 1963. Active state resistance to the decision did not end until the late 1970s. (Klarman, Michael J. *Brown vs Board of Education and the Civil Rights Movement,* Oxford (2007)).

NORTHERN STATES

No northern state had an actual statute requiring segregation of schools. But there was plenty of *de facto* segregation and reaction in many places was not pretty. Although this reminds us that racism is far from just a southern issue the purpose of this book is to demonstrate the waxing and waning of federal vs state power as it relates to people with disabilities. The southern reactions more clearly demonstrate this and that is why they have been chosen. But the north was not innocent. (See DiCara, Lawrence. *Turmoil and Transition in Boston: A Political Memoir of the Busing Era,* Hamilton Books, (2013)). Formisano, Ronald. *Boston against Busing: Race, Class and Ethnicity in the 1960s and 1970s.* University of North Carolina (2004)).

Boston is not the only example. Readers interested in pursuing this subject will find plenty of books and articles on it.

LITTLE ROCK—THE MILITARY ENFORCES BROWN.

The school board of Little Rock, Arkansas had voted to follow *Brown's* desegregation mandate. The questions in Little Rock, as in so many other places, were how and when. After fits and starts Little Rock proposed to integrate its schools consistent with what was called The Blossom Plan. Virgil Blossom, the superintendent of schools, submitted a proposal calling for integration to begin in the fall of 1957 and apply only to one school, Central High School. The second phase of the plan would begin in 1960 and involve a few black children in a few junior high schools. Finally the plan would have integrated the cities grade schools at some unspecified time in the future, possible not until the fall of 1963.

The plan was cautiously accepted by the local NAACP but was quickly changed by the school board to allow inter-district transfer policy. The board had simply gerrymandered the city in a way that guaranteed one of the remaining two high schools would have a large black majority and the other a large white majority. This was particularly distasteful to the black community since it meant bussing their children far from their home school. After negotiations failed the NAACP filed suit against the city in February of 1956.

By the fall of 1957 the NAACP had registered nine black students at previously all white Central High School. These students would come to be known at the "Little Rock Nine." All of them had been screened for histories of good grades and behavior.

The Klan and several segregationist 'councils' threatened to hold demonstrations at Central High to block the black students from entering. Tempers on both sides escalated and on September 4, 1957 Arkansas Governor Orvil Faubus sent the National Guard in support of the segregationist position. Citing his obligation to enforce state laws over federal mandates Faubus deployed armed soldiers to uphold the power of a state against the power of the federal government. Once again that same never-to-go-away issue nearly brought both sides to blows.

School opened with nationally televised images of the "Little Rock Nine" tentatively making their way into school. In the picture were armed combat ready soldiers who supported the segregationists but whose job was to essentially see that the mob did not lynch anyone. For the students it was terrifying. For the nation as a whole it was appalling. In spite of a city wide prayer service and calls from President Eisenhower to Governor Faubus, warning him not to defy federal power, the ugly scenes continued to play out daily.

Finally on September 24 President Eisenhower ordered the 101st Airborne Division to Little Rock to protect the "Little Rock Nine." As a side note all of the divisions black soldiers and officers were pulled from the ranks. They were reunited with their units a month later. No black soldiers deployed to Little Rock. In spite of Eisenhower's action it was still considered too dangerous and provocative to send black soldiers into a southern town.

The President also federalized the entire 20,000 member Arkansas National Guard. Meaning that by his authority as commander in chief he had just inducted the entire Guard into the United States Army. For those soldiers the chain of command no longer ran through Gov. Faubus' office in Little Rock. It now ran through the oval office of now President but former General of the Army Dwight D. Eisenhower. For the segregationists it was both a final insult and a devastating blow.

The year that followed was one of tension and harassment of the Little Rock Nice. One had acid thrown in her face. Another was trapped in a bathroom stall while white students threw burning pieces of paper on her. Verbal threats and minor assaults continued throughout the year as the Little Rock Nine students continued to be escorted to school by soldiers from the 101st Airborne and later the federalized Arkansas National Guard. (Beals, Melba Patillo, *Warriors Don't Cry: The Searing*

Memoir of the Battle to Integrate Little Rock's Central High School. Tantor (1994)).

In the year that followed (known as the 'lost year) Faubus proposed turning Little Rock's school into private academies that could pick and choose its students based on any criteria. That proposal was put to the citizens in a referendum that passed by a large margin. In September of 1958 he closed all the schools in Little Rock causing both white and black students to miss a year.

Faubus' order put teachers in a very difficult position. Those who favored integration were censored and forty four of them were fired for criticism of Faubus. In May of 1959 three segregationist board members were defeated and replaced by moderates. All of the teachers were reinstated. Much to the dismay of Governor Faubus the board reopened the schools in the fall of 1959. Although the 'lost year' came to a close the black students were not welcomed. Everything eventually returned to normal but the legacy contributed to an atmosphere of racial hatred that lasted decades.

In 1999 President Bill Clinton presented each of the students with a Congressional Gold Medal. They attended the inauguration of President Barack Obama at his invitation. The school is now a National Historic site with a civil rights museum recounting the grim tale of nine young people wishing to get a high school education. Seldom has there been a more dramatic example of federal authority used to enforce due process of law. And seldom has there been more determined and racist resistance. (Fitzgerald, Stephanie, (ed.) *The Little Rock Nine: A Struggle for Integration,* Snapshots in History. (1982)). (Anderson, Karen. *Little Rock: Race and Resistance at Central High School.* Princeton. (2010)).

Little Rock was not the end of segregationist resistance to *Brown.* In 1963 Alabama Governor George Wallace 'stood in the schoolhouse door' and famously proclaimed "segregation now, segregation tomorrow, segregation forever.' His last ditch attempt to keep black students out of the University of Alabama spectacularly failed when President Kennedy federalized the Alabama National Guard and ordered them to escort the new students safely to class. Wallace became the darling of segregationists everywhere but his gesture failed. (Clark, E. Culpepper, *The Schoolhouse Door: Segregations Last Stand at the University of Alabama.* Oxford (1995)).

In 1961 an air force veteran named James Meredith, following a successful federal court law suit attempted to register at the University of Mississippi. That state's segregationist governor, Ross Barnett, decreed 'no school will be integrated in Mississippi while I am your Governor." His challenge to federal authority pitted him against Attorney General Robert F. Kennedy who ordered 500 US Marshalls to accompany Meredith who was successfully enrolled. Meredith himself went on to earn a law degree from Columbia University and pursued a very successful career as a civil rights activist. Once again state rights sentiment was forced to back down in the face of federal authority. (Eagles, Charles W. *The Price of Defiance: James Meredith and the Integration of Ole Miss.* Univ. of North Carolina, (2009)).

BROWN CHANGED EVERYTHING.

Brown was a strategic victory that changed everything. No, it did not end racism and segregation. Before *Brown* there was no significant federal effort to interfere in the life of the Jim Crow south. All of the power, prestige and resource of government was on the side, through their state governments, of the segregationists. Virtually overnight that changed.

Suddenly the power of the federal government was on the side of integration. To put it simply prior to the decision if you favored integration you were an outlaw. After the decision your view was the law. Much remained to do and much remains still to do but the opinion added resources, power and the authority of federal courts to the integration struggle. For once the federal government strongly put its power behind enforcement of a Supreme Court opinion that used the 14th Amendment.

In 1999 a different Supreme Court made a similar strategic decision in the case of *L.C. v Olmstead*. Like *Brown* before it is a strategic victory. By ruling that Americans with disabilities have a constitutional right (based on the 14th Amendment) to choose community living over an institution the field changed as dramatically as it did in 1954. Like the earlier case *Olmstead* put the power of the federal government squarely on the side of people favoring community integration. This case did not end segregation of people with disabilities any more than *Brown* ended racism. What it did do was to make community living the law of the land. Like school integration it caused reactionaries of all kinds to go to work figuring out ways to interpret, modify and, if necessary ignore the ruling. But it gave power to those who believe in choice and self-direction. In Part III I will discuss that case in detail and draw parallels with the civil rights movement.

An odd thing about the constitution is that it does not give the Supreme Court any mechanism for enforcing its rulings. There are no police working for the Court. From a ruling onwards it is up to individuals to bring local law suits to force change. More than that implementation requires serious community organizing and political action.

There are many lessons to learn from the Civil Rights Movement that followed *Brown*. The disability rights movement has a similar enforcement responsibility as a result of *Olmstead*. A detailed discussion of those similarities awaits Part III. It is important to recognize the strategic implications of *Olmstead*.

The Civil Rights Movement certainly appreciated the strategic change after *Brown*. I am not going to discuss that movement in any detail tempting though it is. I have dwelt on federal power vs. state rights and the ability of elites to overlook millions of marginalized people be it for race, national origin, gender or disability because that continuing phenomena affects the disability rights movement as much as any other. What I am going to do is a fast summary of the civil rights laws and events that followed *Brown*. Although not destroying racism and prejudice that movement electrified the world with its precision, organization and determination. These are the fruit that can be born when a community organizes to take advantage of a strategic victory.

THE CIVIL RIGHTS MOVEMENT CAPITALIZES ON THE STRATEGIC GAINS OF *BROWN*.

We have seen how the return of Afro-American veterans from WWII, combined with the integration of the armed forces, began a change of attitude among many black people and white people regarding the horrors of the Jim Crow south. Desperation was slowly separating itself from normal lives as a kernel of hope, tentative as it was, began to take root. With *Brown* the whole idea of challenging Jim Crow took on a sense not only of possibility but of hope. And hope is a powerful thing.

MONTGOMERY.

On December 1, 1955 a seamstress named Rosa Parks boarded a public bus in Montgomery, Alabama and took a seat. She would late say "I was tired." Almost immediately she was ordered to give up her seat to a white passenger and move to the back of the bus. She refused, was arrested and sparked a boycott that lasted 381 days.

The morning after her arrest a group of eighteen people met at the Mt. Zion AME Church. The purpose of the meeting was to discuss boycott strategy and to elect a leader for the proposed action. The group chose a minister relatively new to Montgomery and the pastor of the very church they were meeting in. His name was Martin Luther King, Jr.

Following the lead of Mr. King, Ralph Abernathy and others the Afro-American citizens of Montgomery participated in the boycott. People who had ridden the bus for years suddenly walked or organized car pools. Anything but subject themselves to another indignity on buses they paid for with fares and tax dollars.

Predictably the power structure of Montgomery, and the whole South, condemned the boycott as the work of communists, agitators and other villainous elements. Eventually the NAACP sued to have the segregated buses ruled unconstitutional. They federal court ruled that Alabama's racial segregation laws for buses were unconstitutional. Once again the willingness of the court to apply the 14th Amendment served to break down the sense of invincibility that had grown up around segregation and the Jim Crow years. Alabama appealed the decision to the Supreme Court and continued rigid segregation of its buses. But on November 13, 1956 the Supreme Court upheld the lower court and quickly issued an order to Alabama to desegregate its buses. The boycott had worked.

The success of Montgomery breathed new energy and optimism into what was now being called the Civil Rights Movement. The biggest lesson of Montgomery was simple. The People, United, can never be defeated. (Hassler, Alfred. *Martin Luther King and the Montgomery Story,* Top Shelf (2014)). Greenhaw, Wayne. *Fighting the Devil in Dixie: How Civil Rights Activists took on the Ku Klux Klan in Alabama.* Lawrence Hill Books, (2011)).

SELMA

The Supreme Court ruled poll taxes to be unconstitutional. Activists like Medgar Evers and others focused on registering Afro-American voters and had some success. At the same time "Freedom Riders" brought busloads of black and white protesters to the south. The rest of the nation watched in horror as racist crowds greeted the riders with beatings, threats and fire bombs. White supremacists, alarmed at the new activism, resisted any voting by Afro Americans.

Early in 1965 a sheriff in Selma, Alabama decided to clamp down on a black voter registration drive. He arrested and jailed the organizers along with 800 school children. As a result the leaders decided to organize a protest march from Selma to the state capital of Montgomery.

Marching a large mixed race group from Selma to Montgomery meant passing through some of the most racist areas of Mississippi. No one had any illusions about the probability of violence. Nevertheless on March 7, 1965 about 600 civil rights marchers passed through Selma vowing to be true to their pledge of non-violence.

Selma, Alabama is built along both banks of the Alabama River. The Edmund Pettis Bridge spans the river and connects the two sides of the town. The peacefully marching group passed over the bridge and was immediately confronted by a large number of Alabama State Troopers. When the marchers refused orders to turn around the troopers attacked. This may not have been the most brutal racist attack of the era but it most certainly was the first one to be televised, and broadcast over and over. Hundreds of millions of Americans watched in horror as the obviously peaceful marchers were clubbed, beaten, threatened with snarling dogs on chains, pushed by club wielding horsemen and knocked to earth by high pressure hoses. The day was remembered as "Bloody Sunday."

Two days later Dr. King led a large group back to the bridge but, not wanting to violate a court injunction, lead them instead to the safety of the church they had started from. That night James Reeb, a Unitarian Universalist minister from Boston, was beaten to death by a group of racists. More clergy and others flocked to Alabama to support the marchers. All across the nation acts of anti-Alabama civil disobedience occurred.

President Lyndon Johnson had been working behind the scenes to defuse the tension. Alabama officials essentially told him to mind his own business. On March 15 an exasperated Johnson called a joint session of Congress and in an historic nationally televised address asked for the introduction of the Voting Rights Act of 1995.

When Alabama Governor George Wallace made it clear that the marchers were on their own. With a third march scheduled to begin March 21 Johnson, as Eisenhower had done in Little Rock, used the armed authority of the federal government to force a state to comply with federal law. He sent 2,200 soldiers to Selma, federalized 1,100 members of the Alabama National Guard in addition to hundreds of FBI agents and US Marshalls to Selma to protect the marchers and escort them on to Montgomery. On March 25 over 25,000 marchers arrived at the capital in Montgomery in support of voting rights. Their route is now the "Selma to Montgomery National Historic Trail."

...

Author's Note: Selma to Montgomery and the months before and after are events rich in archives, memoires and books. These are the books I used and read for this section. There are many more. Read some.

Branch, Taylor. *Pillar of Fire: America in the King Years 1963-65.* Simon and Schuster (1998).

Combs, Barbara Harris. *From Selma to Montgomery: The Long March to Freedom.* Routledge (2014).

Fager, Charles. *Selma 1965: The March that Changed the South.* Beacon (1985).

King, Coretta Scott. *My Life with Martin Luther King, Jr.* Penguin (1994).

Lewis, John. *Walking with the Wind: A Memoir of the Movement.* Simon and Schuster (1998).

Young, Andrew. *An Easy Burden: The Civil Rights Movement and the Transformation of America.* Baylor University Press, (2004).

—

What is unique about the Selma story is that so many of the Afro-American participants were both the spiritual and, in some cases, genealogical heirs of the slaves that had been counted as 3/5ths of a person at the Constitutional Convention? For eighty years the country had nearly broken up over the question of race. The most deadly war in US History had been fought only to see the legitimate aspirations of millions of slaves crushed by the betrayal of 1876 and the nation turning its back on them during the grim Jim Crow Years. The people who showed up for voting rights were similar to the ADAPT demonstrators who crawled up the steps of the US capital in support of the Americans with Disabilities Act. For both groups oppression had gone on long enough.

Governor's Faubus, Barnett and Wallace are certainly perfect stand-ins to represent the white elites who founded the nation. As we have seen before a conflict over state rights (segregation) and federal power (enforcing the due process clause of the 14th amendment) came face to face. Only the use of federal power allowed the march to continue. Here the pendulum swung in favor of federal power. The states stood down only to grow their bitterness.

The importance of Selma for our purposes is what we can learn about community organizing. The Disability Rights Movement came about as a result of anger, passion, frustration and injustice. It is a sense of shared unhappiness that gives disparate people the motivation necessary to come together in a group and make demands for change. A political movement without direction, leaders and specific goals. Without those things anger and frustration can turn into alienation, frustration and a lingering sense of powerlessness. "You can't fight city hall" is a slogan from a political movement gone bad.

When Rose Parks refused to move to the back of the bus in Montgomery, Alabama her refusal was not a political movement. Her refusal became the catalyst for a political movement when others who had experienced, witnessed or empathized with her action and said 'enough' and came together to end segregation of public transportation. That movement went on to be the Civil Rights Movement that played the key role in the Voting Rights Act of 1965. But without Martin Luther King. Jr, the Southern Christian Leadership Conference, and others to provide organization and leadership the anger likely would have just petered out.

The Disability Rights Movement and the Civil Rights Movement have one thing in common: plenty of anger. But without organization and leadership neither stood or stands a chance of success. It is far easier to block change then it is to achieve it. (For an interesting and brief discussion of political movements and campaigns see: Matthews, Chris. *Hardball: How Politics is Played by One Who Knows the Game.* Penguin. (1999).

THE VOTING RIGHTS ACT OF 1965.

Following the election of 1876 and the rise of Jim Crow the center piece of white power was the denial of voting rights to Afro American citizens. Dr. King and others clearly understood that change was only possible if every citizen enjoyed equal rights in voting. Given that individual states were allowed to set preconditions for voting, poll taxes, literacy tests and when that failed, intimidation and lynching, the only answer left was creation of a federal authority that would take over voting registration, supervise it and give it the authority to change, set aside or remove state voting schemes. Once again our old friend state power vs. federal power clashed in the aftermath of Selma. Current attempts by the right wing to limit registration and suppress voting is as old as the republic.

The Civil Rights Movement had created political conditions ripe for change. President Johnson signed the new law into effect of August 6, 1965. The law specifically forbids literacy and other tests in counties and states where clear evidence of voter discrimination exists. Perhaps more significant was the use of federal power to prohibit states and counties from creating new voter requirements that denied citizens the right to vote. Any proposed change had to be submitted to the Justice Department for approval before taking effect and in all areas covered by the act federal examiners replaced local clerks in registering voters. (See Kousser, J. Morgan. *Colorblind Injustice: Minority Voting Rights and the Undoing of the Second Reconstruction.* Univ. or North Carolina, (1999). Crum, Travis. *The Voting Rights Act's Secret Weapon: Pocket Trigger Litigation and Dynamic Preclearance.* Yale Univ. (2011).

The laws immediate effect was a dramatic increase in Black voter registration. The numbers increased dramatically until Black candidates had a reasonable chance of winning some elections just like they had in the years after the Civil War and before Jim Crow. Using Mississippi as an example 6.4% of black citizens were registered prior to the Voting Rights Act. Five years later 70% were registered. ("Shelby v. Holder". *The New York Times,* June 25, 2013.

An historic outcome of the Voting Rights Act was to turn American politics upside down. At the end of the Civil War republicans were seen as the party of civil rights and federal authority. Democrats were seen as the socially conservative party devoted to the rights of states to do as they wished without regard to the 14th Amendment. Southern voters liked that idea and the 'solid south' was born. Staunchly conservative and pro-segregation the democrats enjoyed the electoral votes of southern states in literally every election beginning in 1880. That was to change.

President Lyndon Johnson, a democrat and a southerner, was seen as a regional, not to mention race, traitor by voters in the south. His support for and signing of a federal law giving voting rights to the despised and marginalized blacks was highly offensive to southern sensibility. Moreover the national Democratic Party was backing the marchers, Dr. King, the new laws and every other thing the Jim Crow hardliners found offensive.

The first presidential election after passage occurred in 1968. The republican nominee was Richard Nixon who clearly saw the road to election in his new 'southern strategy.' Nixon introduced the country to 'wedge issues.' These are issues designed to divide along the lines of race, class and religion.

Nixon's campaign in the south was not so much about telling people what he was for as telling them what he was against. He referred to the enraged racists as the 'silent majority.' He pandered to them with buzz words about 'local control' etc. And for the first time he essentially ran against federal power in Washington. It worked beyond anyone's imagination. He was elected with southern support breaking the hold democrats had held for close to a century. That change is much with us today. Conservative, racist, classist, anti-federalist southern voters now vote as solidly republican as they ever did for democrats. Many working class whites may not vote their own best interests. But they respond positively to rhetoric about 'tyranny' from Washington, outsiders, gays, the disabled, etc. as a threat to them personally. And they vote accordingly. (See *Nixonland: The Rise of a President and the Fracturing of America.* Scribner. (2009)).

In spite of that change Afro-American voters and others with a history of voter discrimination appeared to solidly have the law and the federal power they needed to enjoy the 14th amendments promise of due process and equal justice under law. It appeared that the pendulum had swung decisively in favor of federal power. But in US politics nothing is permanent and nothing is decisive. The old issues of federalism v the rights of states, of a strong constitutional guarantee of equal rights in place of 'local control' were not dead. In some ways they were stronger than ever. In 2013, in a case called *Shelby v Holder,* the old regional resentments scored a major victory when the Supreme Court literally ruled portions of the Voting Rights Act unconstitutional.

With the passage of time and a wholly new and dramatically more conservative Supreme Court the south brought a challenge to Section 4 of the Voting Rights Act. That section concerns a formula the Department of Justice used to determine which counties in states with a history or voter discrimination are subject to federal over site. In order to comply counties were required to submit reports and data each year showing progress in suppressing voter fraud. Failure to do so meant federal supervision of local election offices. Something the southern states resented. Their argument was 'times have changed. Trust us.'

Arguing that 'times have changed' the plaintiffs convinced the Court that these reports were no longer necessary. Alluding to a post-racial society they successfully convinced a majority of justices that further enforcement was an unconstitutional burden on the states. And they struck down that section.

As is true of many Supreme Court cases these days the split was 5-4 along ideological lines. Mr. Chief Justice Roberts, writing for the majority said 'our country has changed and the law in not necessary."

Associate Justice Ruth Bader Ginsburg stingingly wrote in her dissent 'the sad irony of today's decision lies in (the courts) utter failure to grasp why the law has proven so effective." (*NYT,* June 15, 2013.)

The political pendulum had once again swung in the opposite way. In the years between 1965 federal power to assure voting rights was in the ascension. But in 2013 the federal vs state conundrum once again favored the rights of states to interpret and enforce the 14th Amendment as they see fit.

While it is true that other provisions of the law remain in effect it is not impossible for the Justice Department to gather the data necessary to go into southern counties to defend minority voting rights. It is not a coincidence that immediately after *Shelby* state legislatures introduced laws to make it hard or impossible for minorities, the poor, the elderly and the disabled to vote. Under the guise of 'suppressing' and imaginary voter fraud problem it is again problematic to register and vote. One of allegedly more cherished American values.

In 1965 people thought we were well and truly done with voter suppression. With a reasonable federal enforcement procedure in place that seemed a reasonable belief. Today some of the new suppression schemes have been overturned and others upheld. A battle we thought we had fought and won is with us once again.

When Justin Dart, Jr. said 'advocate as if your life depends on it...because it does' he was right.

Today the ability of people with disabilities to participate in and enjoy all of the benefits of citizenship is as at risk as were the freed slaves in 1876. Elites make decisions and continue to be able to overlook the human costs of their competition and folly.

For "Free Our People" to be more than a slogan requires a toughness, a vigilance and a willingness to

lay lives on the line. Without the power of the disability rights movement no individual US citizen with a disability can rely on the permanency of any of the things we need to live full and inclusive lives.
Win together or swing alone.

LITTLE ROCK (AGAIN).

National ADAPT came to Little Rock for its fall action in 2014. Like the civil rights activists of Selma we had traveled great distances to support people with disabilities in Arkansas. The state has one of the most horrid wait lists for basic services (some fifteen years), a great reliance on for profit nursing homes and little or no commitment to community living. All of that could be eliminated if the state adopted a provision of the Affordable Care Act called the community first choice option. We too marched. This time in support of people with disabilities.

For three days we walked the streets under a blistering southern sun. We visited the office of the governor, the nursing home lobby headquarters, and office of the so called "Americans for Prosperity" as well as the campaign headquarters of the major party candidates for governor. Although the people of Little Rock generally greeted us warmly not so the police. Nearly 200 of us were arrested amidst a constantly changing set of rules. One day on the sidewalk and arrested for being in the street. Next day arrested for being on the side walk instead of the street. Arkansas media gave great daily coverage. We believed we did all we could do to educate people about the conditions our disabled brothers, sisters and friends are forced to live with. "ADAPT Does Little Rock" was seen everywhere.

The day after the action Amber Smock and I visited the Little Rock Central High School National Historic Site. Central High School still operates and looks much as it does in the photographs and grainy newsreel film. The center itself, run by the National Park Service, tells the integration story very well. Photos of white segregationists, their faces contorted with anger screaming at the children. Faces of frightened young soldiers and pictures and words memorializing the dignity and grace and courage of the students.

History was close that morning and we both felt we were on hallowed ground. We were walking in the footsteps of The Little Rock Nine. We were both feeling pretty emotional and very lucky to be there.

After a period of looking at the exhibits and chatting with the park rangers one of us saw another exhibit. This one dedicated to the men and women of the disability rights movement. Some words below the famous photograph of a line of ADAPT people in wheel chairs and all dominated by a giant unfurled ADAPT flag. As we got nearer we knew the photo had been taken by our friend Tom Olin.

The person wielding the giant flag was our comrade Tom Wilson. We knew just about everyone in the photo. We stood silently. Both of us were each feeling quite emotional to see our people, our flag, equated with the Little Rock Nine. We both felt how right that was. We both felt very at home in that time and place. Free Our People was more than a slogan to us. It was in our hearts, our souls, and our commitment.

We were comfortable, proud and not afraid.

For some reason as I stood there I remembered text carved in granite from the World War II Memorial in Washington, DC. The words floated through my mind.
"They had no right to win. Yet they did.
Even against the greatest of odds. There is something special in the human spirit,
A magical blend of skill, faith and valor—
That can lift us from certain defeat to incredible victory."

We stood in silence, each in the privacy of own thoughts. Each of us suppressing a sob. Then we turned away from the photo and from one another and walked out of the center. In the footsteps of giants. But confident that we knew the truth.

Same struggle…different difference.

PART 2

Here to Stay

"My members are into confrontation. We'll tell somebody what we want, and we'll talk about it once or twice, but that's it. Then we deal with you. Either we shut you down or whatever."
Wade Blank

"We are all answerable for the empowerment of others."
Amber R. Smock

Disability is natural. People with intellectual and developmental disabilities have been a part of humanity from the beginning. That is not in contention. What is contentious is the reception these newly born humans received upon arrival.

The Egyptian Papyrus of Thebes dates from 1552 BCE and contains the first references to people with intellectual and developmental disability. The Classical civilizations of Greece and Rome regarded these births as evidence that the gods had been angered. Mostly these children were killed at birth or left to die of exposure. Few were ever allowed to grow up. The one exception was the Roman custom of allowing property rights and guardians to people with intellectual and developmental disability born to wealthy families. As time passed more and more babies were allowed to live so long as they were protected and kept out of sight by their families or, if the family could afford it, by monasteries. In some cases people born with what were perceived as severe intellectual disability were believed to have the ability to receive and interpret divine revelation. (Harris, J.C. 2006. *Intellectual disability: understanding its development, causes, classification, evaluation and treatment.* New York. Oxford University Press.)

When delegates from the thirteen disparate colonies met in Philadelphia during May of 1787 not much had changed in the world's view of people with intellectual and developmental disabilities. There is no evidence to suggest that people with any kind of disability were considered at all in those proceedings. In the regard they were just like natives and women. No one considered anyone but white male property owners to have a say in the formation of the new government and that government, in its turn, considered the desires and well-being of those property owners to be its very reason to exist.

As we have seen the millions of slaves were considered. Considered worthy of counting as three-fifths of a person in apportioning the House of Representatives. But, like the other excluded groups were certainly not considered worthy of rights, representation or membership in the new nation.

Certainly there is no reason to believe that the proportion of disabled and non-disabled people was any different in 1787. The delegates certainly were not ignorant of their disabled countrymen and women. But the convention was interested in other things and willing to ignore or overlook millions of people based on gender, race and disability. To large degree the founders seem to have thought of their strip of land along the Atlantic Ocean as a free market where goods, services and the creation of wealth could move from the Canadian border to the Caribbean Sea without tariffs, local fees or interference. Before adopting the constitution they insisted on adding amendments (now called The Bill of Rights) and the first one provided for freedom of religion. Did keeping protestants and Catholics from slaughtering each other in the name of faith done for altruistic reasons or simply because the delegates had witnessed the negative impact on business of the endless European religious wars? Motivation aside the document is heavy on commerce and weak on inclusion. Add the flowery language of the French enlightenment and the stage was set for a double standard of what is said being far from what is done that has stayed with the republic to this day.

Like slaves and the disabled, Native Americans were ignored too. Even the basic notion of them having rights and a culture deserving of respect and protection never occurred to any of the delegates. Instructive that it took an act of Congress to guarantee them the right to religious freedom including the right to practice it with the use of and possession of objects considered sacred. (See American Indian Religious Freedom Act, 92 Stat. 469 (1979)

The first program of intervention for intellectual disability appeared in France in 1799. Edward Seguin, a disciple of the program's developer Jean-Mark Itard, took the methods further and established a program for the 'feeble minded' in Paris. The program emphasized some new elements such as individual instruction and behavior management which are still practiced. After immigrating to the United States Sequin published an influential book (*Idiocy and Its Treatments in Physiological Methods)* that has impacted thinking for generations. In 1841 the first residential facility for people with intellectual disability was established in Switzerland by Johann Guggenbuhl. It was called "Adenburg" and is credited with being the prototype for institutional care. A model still much with us. (See, Harbour, C. K., Maulik PK (2010). History of Intellectual Disability. In JH Stone, M Blouin, editors. International Encyclopedia of Rehabilitation).

In July, 1848 about four hundred delegates gathered at Seneca Falls, New York to address the needs of another group left out of the constitution. Participants included Cady Elizabeth Stanton and the Philadelphia based Lucretia Mott a fiery Quaker orator. Susan B. Anthony was in attendance along with the abolitionist Frederick Douglas. With Douglas' participation the conference included two excluded groups. For the first time both women and Afro-Americans claimed the rights guaranteed their white, male property owning countrymen. There is no record of anyone with a disability attending or even being mentioned. It would take until 1919 for the first woman to vote. Oddly Douglas and his abolitionist message only had to wait until 1865 and the passage of the thirteenth amendment. Douglas had vowed never to separate the two issues but quite readily tossed the woman's movement under the proverbial bus to address the politics of abolishing slavery. He and Stanton never again spoke. (Huggins, Nathan Irvin and Handlin, Oscar. *Slave and Citizen: The Life of Frederick Douglas.* Library of America. 1980)

Seneca Falls is not our story. But it does informally mark the beginning of a period of United States history characterized by social movements that were based on an optimistic view of human nature. This was a period of thought that would last until the end of the nineteenth century. People with intellectual and developmental disabilities were suddenly thought capable of being rehabilitated, trained and perhaps even integrated into main stream society. (Beirne-Smith, M. Patton, Jr. and Kim, SH. *Mental Retardation: An introduction to intellectual disabilities.* Prentice Hall. 2006). The 'reformist era', as it is called, would turn out to have profound impact on the lives of people with disabilities. Impacts that may have had the best of intentions but lead to some very painful and wrong-headed outcomes.

Born in 1802 Dorothea Dix was raised in a home with an abusive alcoholic father. During her childhood she and her mother were forced to flee their home in Worchester, Massachusetts and seek safety in Boston. An incident that influenced her later reform zeal. She was particularly passionate about the plight of what she called the 'indigent insane' as well as inmates in jails and prisons. Dix spoke, agitated and traveled widely including an influential time in Liverpool, England with a wealthy Quaker family. Through them she became acquainted with the 'lunacy reform' movement in England. During the United States Civil War she was appointed Superintendent of Army nurses where she earned the ire of her superiors by insisting that confederate wounded be treated with the same kindness and care as the union soldiers were.

In the world of people with disabilities she is most known for her role in establishing the first public mental hospital in the country. The Pennsylvania State Lunatic Hospital operated in Harrisburg from 1851 to 1937. The hospital was built with public funds and accepted patients from all parts of the state. Their cost, if they were indigent, were covered by their home counties. A 130 acre farm was established adjacent to the institution itself. There, it was believed, the 'lunatics' could benefit from hard farm work and the healthy food they grew. Eventually over seventy buildings were erected. Considered progressive at the time the 'cottage system' was first devised here. Based on current best practice patients were carefully segregated by sex and lived in group cottages located near the center of the campus. That model would be adopted by institutions in every state and eventually be the background for the hundreds of thousands of disabled people who lived out their lives is the splendid isolation of a rural farm far from disapproving eyes and far from mainstream American life. For better or for worse the institutional care model was now the sacrosanct altar upon which the lives of others were mandated. (Golloher, David L. *Voice for the Mad: A Life of Dorothea Dix*. Bidwell. 1995).

Samuel Gridley Howe was born in Boston in 1801. In 1824 he graduated from Harvard Medical School and prepared to practice as a Boston physician. Howe was a young man with a lot on his mind besides medicine. Just before he opened his practice an unhappy love affair and the involvement of his hero Lord Byron in the Greek Civil War caused him to go to Greece where he enrolled as a surgeon in the insurgent army. He returned to Boston to raise funds and went back to Greece. Technically a surgeon Howe's experience was not limited to medicine. His courage under fire and leadership abilities caused him to become known as "the Lafayette of the Greek Revolution." By now a strong adherent of representative democracy Howe went to Paris to continue his medical studies and while there participated in the July Revolution of 1828. (Schwartz, Harold. *Samuel Gridley Howe, Social Reformer 1801-1876*. Harvard University Press, 1956).

In 1831 Howe was invited by a group of Boston reformists to return home and found and direct a new philanthropic institution to be known as the New England Asylum for the Blind. Howe left immediately for Europe where he learned all he could at the Paris School for the Blind founded by Valentin Huey. In 1784 Huey had founded the Royal Institution for the Young Blind in Paris.

It was the first such school in the world and in 1819 a young blind man named Louis Braille enrolled. Over a period of years a method of printing that could be read digitally by blind people was developed. This method became known as Braille in honor of the first person to learn to use it effectively. (Weygand, Zina. *The Blind in French Society from the Middle Ages to the Century of Louis Braille.* Stanford University. 2009).

Howe returned to Boston in 1833 fired by a new enthusiasm by what he had seen and learned in Paris about the possibility of educating the blind. This reformist spirit of optimism fit right into the political agitation in Boston which increasingly included calls for the abolition of slavery. He became so close to the abolitionist John Brown that when Brown was executed for treason following his raid on the federal arsenal in Harpers Ferry, West Virginia Howe fled to Canada for a time to avoid possible prosecution. Eventually he married Julia Howe whose family was staunchly abolitionist and who wrote the words to the *Battle Hymn of the Republic.*

The constitution had ignored the needs of women, slaves and the disabled. By the time Howe returned to Boston the three groups had already begun to be drawn together. Certainly the abolition of slavery and women's suffrage emerged with leaders determined to create their own future. But when it came to disability no voice was heard. The reform, education, rehabilitation and improvement of the lives of Americans with disabilities was something about to be done to them. Not with them. A notion that has sadly stayed with us to this day.

Howe's effort, like that of the other reformers was financially based on a sort of 'white man's burden' philanthropy. In 1833 a wealthy Bostonian whose fortune came from trade in slaves and opium, Thomas

Perkins, donated his mansion as a location for the school 'in perpetuity.' After a few years that building was found unsuitable and Perkins consented to its sale. The proceeds were used to purchase a new location in South Boston where the school was renamed the Perkins School for the Blind.

By 1837 the Perkins School had begun to lay the foundation for the education of the blind by taking in blind/deaf students. In 1837 Laura Bridgeman, a young deaf blind girl enrolled at Perkins and was instructed by Howe himself. She became famous in her own right as the first known deaf/blind person in the United States to learn to read and write using a manual alphabet. Bridgeman went on to become a teacher at Perkins Institute. (*Perkins Annual Reports,* retrieved from the internet, September 7, 2015).

In March of 1887 one of Bridgeman's students, Anne Sullivan, was sent from Boston to the small town of Tuscumbia in northwestern Alabama. The deaf/blind child she was sent there to work with was named Helen Keller. The collaboration between Ann Sullivan and Helen Keller is of course a story well told in *The Miracle Worker* by William Gibson.

In 1888 Keller came to Boston and enrolled in the Perkins School. There she learned to write and read using braille and a manual alphabet. She earned degrees, wrote a book in German, became an outspoken democratic socialist and the most famous disabled person in the world. Keller was still very much alive in 1956 and presided at the dedication of the Keller-Sullivan Building which housed the school deaf/blind education program. (Keller, Helen *The Story of My Life.* Bantam. 1990). See also (Davidson, Margaret. *Helen Keller.* Scholastic Books, 1989).

In 1848 Howe, working with Dorothea Dix founded the "Massachusetts School for Idiot and Feeble Minded Youth." Howe's success in educating young people with intellectual and developmental disabilities was so great that other reformers began to agitate for the idea that since these students did so well at Howe's school that they should permanently reside there.

To his credit Howe did object to that notion and advocated reintegration into the community.

But by then the damage was done.

The institutionalization of Americans with developmental disabilities had begun. A wrong-headed notion that is still with us to this day. The reformist guns were now firmly aimed at Americans with intellectual disabilities. A lot was about to happen to them. Everyone agreed it was all for their own good. Everyone but the actual people impacted. No one asked them. (Pleiffer, David. *Samuel Gridley Howe and Schools for the Feeble Minded.* The Ragged Edge. Retrieved from the Internet, September 7, 2015). See also (Trent, James W. *The Manliest Man: Samuel G. Howe and the Contours of Nineteenth Century American Reform.* University of Massachusetts. 2013).

Another example of progressive era philosophy, sociology, suffrage and activism is Jane Addams. Born in Illinois in 1860 she was a member of a politically prominent family. Her father was a bank president, a founder of the republican party of Illinois and a close friend of Abraham Lincoln who made a fortune in timber holdings, timber speculation and various mills and small factories. Her childhood was one of affluence and optimism.

A voracious reader the works of *Dickens* had a great influence on her and she resolved to become a doctor in order to help the poor. Her father insisted that she attend college near home and in 1881 she graduated from Rockport Female Seminary (now Rockford University). Using an inheritance from her father she and her sister moved to Philadelphia to attend medical school. After one year of medical training Addams experienced health issues, spinal surgery and what was then called a 'nervous breakdown'. She returned to Chicago full of sadness regarding her health and her perceived failure to complete medical school. (Knight, Louise W. *Citizen: Jane Addams and the Struggle for Democracy.* University of Chicago Press. 2005).

At this point in her life she was heavily influenced by three books. Tolstoy's *My Religion* awakened her to the struggles of early Christians. At the time Giuseppe Manzini's *Duties of Man* was highly influential with others of her social circle and she began to think of democracy not so much as a system of government but as a social idea. During this period of her 'nervous breakdown' she seriously questioned the confusion surrounding her role as a woman. John Stuart Mill's *The Subjection of Women* caused her to doubt the pressures on women to marry and devote their lives to family and children. (Knight, Louise W. *Citizen.* Pp 142-148). She concluded that failure to complete medical school did not preclude her from other actions on behalf of the poor and began to think in terms of some kind of settlement house as a kind of neighborhood resource center, kitchen, library and support as needed. After much thought she settled on the turbulent neighborhoods of south Chicago.

In 1889 Addams and a college friend who became her lifelong companion founded a settlement house in a rundown mansion on Chicago's south side. They named it Hull House after the man who had built it some forty years before. (Addams, Jane. *20 Years at Hull-House.* Univ. of Chicago, 2013).

By the beginning of the twentieth century an eclectic mix of immigrants from Eastern Europe had settled in Chicago. Their neighborhoods had little or no municipal services. Disease was rampant as were prostitution, extortion, and all the social ills one associates with overcrowded spaces and abject poverty. "Germans and Jews resided south of 12th Street. The Greek Delta formed by Harrison, Halsted and Blue Island Streets served as a buffer to the Irish residing to the north and the Canadian French to the northwest. Italians resided within the inner core of the Hull House neighborhood...from the river to the east end, on out to the western ends of what became known as Little Italy." (*Stories from Chicago's Little Italy.* Taylor Street Archives. Retrieved from the internet Sept. 15, 2015.)

At its height Hull House was a residence for twenty-five women and had 2,000 visitors a week. Residents conducted investigations of housing, fatigue, midwifery, tuberculosis, typhoid, garbage, cocaine and truancy. There was a night school for adults, art gallery, children's clubs, a gym, a public kitchen, a girl's club, as well as a bath house, bookbindery, drama group, theater, a music school, library with meeting rooms, employment bureau and a lunch room. (Lundblad, Karen Shaffer, *Jane Addams and Social Reform: A Role Model for the 1990s.* Social Work. 1995).

Hull House was gradually dragged into the political arena. Addams and her compatriots advocated for reforms at the municipal, state and federal levels. They made significant contributions to reformist agendas regarding such issues as health care, women's suffrage, child labor and immigration policy. Indeed many observers believe that Hull House marked the beginning of what is not known as social work. (Jackson, Shannon. *Lines of Activity Performance, Historiography, Hull House Domesticity.* University of Michigan, 2001).

Although Hull House was not specifically a disability service provider there is no doubt that among its neighbors were people with every kind of disability. At the time there was not yet a system of diagnosis, segregation, treatment and separate lives. People with disabilities were just another part of the great drama of human life. Where Addams does talk specifically about disability her thoughts are aimed primarily at children.

"The first three crippled children we encountered in the neighborhood had all been injured while their mothers were at work: one had fallen out of a third story window, another had been burned and a third had a curved spine due to the fact that for three years he had been tied all day long to the leg of a kitchen table, only released at noon by his older brother who hastily ran in from a neighboring factory to share his lunch with him. Hull House was thus committed to a day nursery which we maintained for sixteen years." (Addams, Jane. Twenty Years at Hull House. Biblio. 1999).

Adams was a champion of blacks, immigrants, working women, children the sick and poor. She was also a pacifist who opposed US entry into WW I and eventually because the first woman to win the Nobel Peace Prize. Significantly she also supported research into the causes of poverty, illness and social disconnect. Clearly people with disabilities were included in all of those categories although, as yet, not segregated into special categories of treatment, care and rehabilitation.

In all of this Addams was typical of the early to late-1800s optimism that prevailed as regards the chances of successful rehabilitation, training and integration of people with disabilities into normal life. As we have seen Dorothea Dix, Samuel Gridley Howe and others struggled against poorhouses, alms houses, asylums, country homes and in favor of specialized institutional settings for the 'treatment' of people with disabilities. That was all well and good until the optimism of the early 1800s waned with the realization that whatever one did for, and or to, people with disabilities the one thing that could not be done is to make them 'normal'. Normalcy was an accepted value. Abnormal was not. In a few short years the prism of reform switched from protection, charity and pity to a far more sinister view of disability, and especially intellectual disability, into viewing it all as a problem in need of a fix. Seeing disability as simply something to be combatted, feared and eliminated the reformist zeal came up with some solutions that were to bring unspeakable horror on the community. The age of eugenics and institutionalization dawned.

As the 19th Century moved along the population of the U.S. began to become more and more urbanized. A trend that continues to this day. As more and more people were joined together in large groups people with intellectual and physical disability were more *and* more visible and more on the reformist radar. An industrialized, urban country where employment depended more and more on intellectual capability and less and less on physical ability soon convinced itself that people with intellectual disabilities were far less able to conform their conduct to the requirements of this new industrial age.

Howe, Dix, Addams and others put faith in the value of training, rehabilitation and integration of all into society but their disciples were soon disillusioned by the fact that people with intellectual disability could certainly be taught skills but by no means could they be made 'normal.' This failure lead to a diluting of the traditional training and rehabilitation model to more and more reliance on residential institutions. Suddenly people with intellectual disability, who up until now had just been part of the world we occupy, became known as the feebleminded. Being different of course provoked fear and it was not long before they were blamed for the poverty, illness and crime that characterized urbanization. Tuberculosis, prostitution, poverty and slums as well as disability were thought to be inherited traits. The logical remedy was to eliminate the possibility that people with disability could reproduce thus slowly eliminating the undesirable element from society. (Beirne-Smith, M. *Mental Retardation: An introduction to intellectual disabilities.* Prentice Hall, 2006).

This irrational fear of intellectual disability is permanently enshrined in the American psyche by John Steinbeck's novel *Of Mice and Men.* In the book George Milton and Lennie Small live in a migrant camp in California during the great depression. Both of them share a dream of owning their own land and are fast friends. Lennie loves to stroke kittens and spends many happy hours doing so. As fate would have it the wife of a character enters a barn when Lenny is petting a kitten and discovering his love for soft things suggests he stroke her hair. He does but she becomes alarmed and screams that she is being raped. Lennie barely escapes the mob and his friend George takes him to a safe play to die a painless death. Lennie, the gentle man with an intellectual disability has become the archetype of the crazed, sex obsessed, mentally retarded fiend who terrorizes decent folk and needs both to be feared and kept a safe distance. A perception still held by many. (Steinbeck, John. *Of Mice and Men,* Library of America. 2008).

In 1869 Francis Galton, a cousin of Charles Darwin, published a book that would become the theoretical foundation for the eugenics movement. Galton argued persuasively that nature and natural selection formed the basis for human personality and nature. He discounted totally the possible role of poverty, disease, nurture, education and nutrition. If this were true then the undesirable traits could be completely and totally eliminated simply by controlling who could and who could not reproduce. By reducing the number of human breeding couples to only those with the desired traits of success and socialization eventually all social evil could be eliminated. Like many bad ideas it sounded good at the time. (Galton, Francis. *Hereditary Genius: An Inquiry into its laws and consequences.* Biblio. 2010).

Just how 'intellectuals' became disciples of something as grotesque as eugenics is a good question. Two popular and influential books certainly helped set the stage for the consensus that grew around the idea of forced sterilization.

The first of these, published in 1877 was *The Jukes: A Study in Crime, Pauperism, Disease and Heredity (London, Bantam).* This was followed in 1912 by *The Kalliak Affair: A Study of in the Heredity of Feeble-Mindedness.* (Boston, 1912). Both the books and their numerous followers concluded that modern medicine and social reform interfered with Darwinian natural selection. Their conclusion was that people with intellectual or mental disability were reproducing faster than valuable productive people and were to blame for the cost of prisons, schools, hospitals and institutions. See also (Rosen, Christine. *Preaching Eugenics: Religious Leaders and the American Eugenics Movement.* Oxford University Press, 2004.)

In 1907 Indiana became the first US state to adopt a eugenics law. It called for the forced sterilization of "imbeciles" who had been diagnosed as "unimproveable." (Reilly, Philip. *The Surgical Solution: A History of Involuntary Sterilization in the United States.* Princeton.

1991). By 1944, thirty states had sterilization laws. (Sofair, AN, Kaldihian, LC. *Eugenic Sterilization and a qualified Nazi analogy: The United States and Germany 1930-1945.* The Annals of Internal Medicine 132(4).

Between 1907 and 1944 more than 42,000 people were forcibly sterilized in the United States in an attempt to eliminate the presumed genetic causes of disease including feeblemindedness. From 1943 to 1983 and additional 22,000 were sterilized in 27 different states in an attempt to prevent intellectual disability and other conditions thought to be heritable. (Sofair).

By 1927 the notion of selective breeding was so deeply entrenched in United States social practice that even the Supreme Court got into the act. Mr. Justice Oliver Wendell Holmes, Jr., writing for the court, ruled that a 'state statute permitting compulsory sterilization of the unfit, including the intellectually disabled, for the protection and health of the state, does not violate the due process clause of the Fourteenth Amendment." *Beck v. Bell.* 274 US 200 (1927). The case has never been specifically overruled.

In my own state of Oregon more than 2,000 residents of the Fairview Training Center were forcibly sterilized. Until the late 1970s release into the community required a vasectomy, forced hysterectomies, tubal ligations and even castration. In a rare recognition of the human cost Dave Reynolds of Inclusion Daily Express reported the following story from the point of view of a victim.

"-Kenneth Richard Newman is not exactly sure how old he was when his parents left him at Fairview Training Center, but he does remember what happened that day.

"My parents took me out to Fairview, and hopped in the car and left," says Newman, now 59. "I was just standing there, going, what happened? It's like a gateway to hell opened up."

Now, Newman and his wife Shirley, who also lived at Fairview, are asking for an apology for their incarceration, the abuse they endured, and the trickery that was used to sterilize them. "What they told me is this is your release papers. They said, you're gonna get out in the community...They whipped them out and said, 'Sign here.'"

"I feel like I've been robbed, I've been cheated. I didn't ask for this to happen," adds Newman.

"It was terrible, living in a place like that, an institution," explains Shirley Newman. "I never did anything wrong."

Oregon had adopted a eugenics law in 1913 and in 1923 a Board of Eugenics. Later called the Board of Social Protection it existed until 1983. In December 2002 Governor John Kitzhaber formally apologized for the program noting 'a great wrong was done to Oregonians.' (*British Medical Journal* 325 (7377) Dec. 14, 2002).

By the 1930s the US eugenics program was so enshrined and 'successful' that it attracted the attention of Adolf Hitler and the Nazis. It is well documented that Hitler's T-34 Program, which rounded up and actually murdered people with intellectual disabilities, was first inspired by the US model. Even the Rockefeller Foundation got in the Hitler act by providing him grants that helped develop a fund Nazi eugenics programs. US intellectuals and social reformists were proud of the influence they played with Hitler as demonstrated by this quote from C. M. Goethe, a leader of the eugenics movement in California. Upon his return from Germany in 1934 he wrote this to a colleague.

"You will be interested to know that your work has played a powerful part in shaping the opinions' of a group of intellectuals who are behind Hitler in this epoch-making program. Everywhere I sensed that their opinions have been tremendously stimulated by American thought...I want you, my dear friend, to carry this thought with you for the rest of your life, that you have really jolted into action a great nation of 60 million people." (Kuhl, Stephan. *The Nazi Connection: Eugenics, American Racism and German National Socialism.* Oxford University, 2015).

Eventually over 300,000 people with intellectual and developmental disabilities would be murdered in Hitler's T-34 Program. (Spitz, Vivian. *Doctors from Hell: The Horrific Account of Nazi Experiments on Humans.* Sentinent. 2005.) Although change of thought was slow the embarrassment of US eugenic program contributing to the opening stages of the Holocaust certainly played a role in helping to end the practice in the US.

Forced sterilization of course required a method of identifying appropriate subjects. Once again good intentions backfired on our community with the development of psychological testing to diagnose abnormality, disability or undesirable traits. In 1905 Alfred Binet and Theodore Simon developed a test in France for identifying schoolchildren who were considered in need of special services. (Beirne, et al 2006). Intelligence tests were first developed by the US Army during both World Wars in hope of effectively assigning personnel. These tests identified people with intellectual disabilities and made them appear more numerous than they are in fact. It is psychological testing and research in eugenics which stimulated the development of qualitative methods in the US. (Radford, JP. *Sterilization versus Segregation, Control of the 'Feebleminded" 1900-1938.* Annals of Internal Medicine 134. 2000.) These tests represent the beginning the labeling so hated by people with intellectual disability and so revered by those who try to manage and control them.

The philosophical foundation of eugenics is the belief in hereditary traits being concentrated in a relatively small group who pass them along from one generation to the next perpetuating intellectual disability as well as poverty, crime, etc. (As Justice Holmes famously noted in *Bell* "three generations of idiots is enough.") By the 1930s and 1940s non-genetic factors such as health care, environment, nutrition, etc. refuted the single cause explanations common in eugenics. Studies of individuals in institutions established that more than half of them had parents without intellectual disability. (Bierne-Smith et al. 2006.) Other studies established that people with intellectual disability were born in about the same proportion in all parts of society and were not concentrated in the lowest social orders as the eugenicists had insisted. (Reilly, 1987). Opposition from the Catholic Church, new research, the proximity of US eugenics to Nazi extermination discredited the underpinning of eugenics.

By the early 1960s most states had abandoned their eugenics program. In 1974 North Carolina, which had sterilized more than 7,600 of its citizens, became the last state to repeal its eugenics law. (Winston-Salem Journal. *N.C. Last state to stop eugenics may be the first to compensate victims.* Retrieved from the internet Sept. 25, 2015). By then over 70,000 people had been forcibly sterilized. For them the end came too late.

As the faux-science of eugenics was gradually discredited and the practice discontinued its attitude and paternalism gave rise to something even more sinister for people with disabilities. A medical model (or deficit model) of disability replaced eugenics as the number one barrier to the quality of life for people with disability. Unlike eugenics it is very much with us today.

This medical model looks upon disability as something akin to illness. Like an illness disability needs to be cured or fixed. This model focuses on the individual's limitations and ponders ways to reduce them. What it does not do is accept the normalcy of disability and the role that society and appropriate supports may play in a person's quality of life. The person with the disability is seen as somehow defective and in need of help, interventions and cure.

Advocates of course argue that a social model is more real and far more appropriate. A medical or deficit model of disability has unintentionally (perhaps) led to social degradation and perpetual infantilism disabled persons. Among the many criticisms leveled at this model is the waste of resources in medical, surgical, social or occupational cures and treatments. Resources that could better be used on things like universal design of buildings and socially inclusive practices such as supported employment, home care, public transportation and affordable health care. Most of the people currently involved in the modern disability rights movement regard the medical model as a civil rights issue. One that portrays disabled people as pitiable, negative, and largely disempowered and badly in need of intervention, help and supervision. The social model casts people with disability as a political, social and environmental issue. In short it believes that people with disabilities are just fine as they are. Alan Holdsworth (aka Johnny Crescendo) has perhaps best summed up the attitude disabled people share toward the medical model with his slogan "piss on pity."

The medical model is often pointed to by contemporary critics as the basis for what has come to be known as the Disability/Industrial Complex. That is a vast set of non-disabled people and interests who dominate the service system as they deem appropriate. Most commonly in a way that benefits their agency, program or funding source. Most notable is its total lack of interest in what people with disabilities might have to say. Here it is useful to fall back on an old journalism phrase "follow the money."

"The following groups all benefit from disability: physicians and all other medical personnel who treat people with disabilities: the entire health care field, from policymakers to nursing home conglomerates to HMOs: lawyers, who prosecute and defend personal injury, custody and discrimination cases: the 'helping' professions, psychologists to social workers to special education teachers, bureaucracies, such as social security agencies, welfare departments, the Veteran's Administration, industries, such as wheelchair manufacturers, vehicle modification businesses, and adaptive equipment makers: foundations, associations and charities that raise money: research about (and sometimes on) people with disabilities and academics who teach and write about disability issues: people who own stocks in companies that benefit from the business or serving (or exploiting, depending on your viewpoint) people with disabilities: and myriad other groups who owe their employment to us, including rehabilitation agencies, art centers and people, like myself, who make a living consulting, writing and talking to groups of people with disabilities." (Brown, Stephen E. *Movie Stars and Sensuous Scars: Essays on the Journey from Disability Shame to Disability Pride.* iUniverse, Inc. (2003).

Dr. Brown's list is consistent with what Paul Longmore called disabled versus non-disabled interests. When evaluating a program, system or proposal he suggests always asking 'who benefits? Is it us or is it our keepers?' (Longmore, Paul. *Why I Burned my book and other essays on disability.* Temple University. 2003)

"The medical approach, by typically regarding disabled people as patients or dependent objects of charity, has thereby rendered them historically inert or invisible. Older histories of 'the deaf' or 'the blind' made them passive recipients of the benevolence of those regarded as the real historical agents: hearing or sighted professionals and philanthropists... In many fields of historical inquiry where disability was significant, the medical pathology perspective has located the causes of alleged social incapacity within 'afflicted' individuals, thereby excluding consideration of cultural, social and political factors in the construction of disabled people's identities and roles and overlooking disabled people as historical actors." (Longmore, p 56.) See also (Lane, Harlan. *The Mask of Benevolence: Disabling the Deaf Community.* Dawn Sign Press. 1999).

The medical model of disability is a civil rights issue. Advocates rightly object to charitable or even medical events that portray people with disabilities as pitiable, negative, disempowered and badly in need of drastic interventions to be determined by non-disabled interests. The disability rights movement has argued for years that to whatever degree disability is a 'problem' it is one to be viewed a political, social and environmental. The medical model by non-disabled people and interests and is impossible to meet. From this has come modern slogans and resistance such as 'disability is natural,' 'label jars not people' and 'my biggest disability is your attitude.'

This quixotic search for 'normalcy', along with a desire to control reproduction, lead to the institutional model of segregating people with disabilities, often from birth to death, in large institutions. Regardless of how attractive and pastoral these institutions look they all have one thing in common. All of them are custodial. People with intellectual and developmental disabilities, being seen alternatively as a genetic threat or in need of childlike life span care, are simply removed from society.

The numbers of people who have been incarcerated in state institutions is huge. In 1848, about the time the first people were institutionalized there were ten people identified as residing in one. By the end of the 19th Century that number begin to grow rapidly. By 1938 97,209 Americans with intellectual or developmental disabilities were isolated in 'out of sight out of mind' institutions. The number peaked in 1967 when 194,650 were counted in state run institutions.

As the deinstitutionalization movement gained steam the numbers have declined but are still enormous. In 2013 there were still 24,675 people institutionalized and only two states had completely eliminated the practice. (Braddock, et. al. *State of the States,* Coleman Institute and Department of Psychiatry, University of Colorado. 2014.)

Although some families made an effort to maintain contact with their institutionalized child most were convinced by doctors and other 'experts' that the best thing they could do is simply send their disabled baby to an institution and pretend they were ever born. How many children, youth and adults were thereby deprived of family contact and traditions will never be known. In part because of the abandonment the residents lost any kind of political power or voice. As a result they were/are often underfunded, overcrowded and unsafe.

The Fairview Training Center in my own state of Oregon closed in 2000. When it did stories surfaced of residents being tied to steam pipes in dark tunnels, whipped, tied in leather cuffs, razor straps, cow whips and isolation cells. (Oregon Dept., of Human Services. 2002). Others told stories of overcrowding, lack of privacy and shoddy medical care such as have damaged joints fused instead of repaired. Thrifty minded administrators were happy with the fusing since it was cheaper than repair. Of course no one asked the residents whose arms and legs would no longer bend. During its existence Fairview witnessed over 2,000 forced sterilizations, vasectomies, forced hysterectomies, tubal ligations and castrations. Fairview was in no way unique. Abuse, neglect, no education, poor nutrition characterized every year of its existence.

Another example is the Willowbrook State 'School' located on Staten Island in New York City. Opened in 1947 the school expanded to a maximum capacity of 4,000. But by 1965 its population exceeded 6,000. Conditions were unspeakable although no one seemed to care until Senator Robert F Kennedy toured the school in 1965 and declared residents of the overcrowded facility were "living in filth and dirt, their clothing in rags, in rooms less comfortable and cheerful than the cages in which we put animals in a zoo." Kennedy went on to characterize the institution as a snake pit. (*Excerpt from statement by Sen. Kennedy.* The New York Times, Sept. 10, 1965. Retrieved from the internet September 28, 2015).

Kennedy's expose attracted the attention of a young reported named Geraldo Rivera. In 1972 he conducted a series of investigations at Willowbrook uncovering a host of deplorable conditions including overcrowding, lack of sanitation, and physical and sexual abuse by members of the schools staff. Rivera's expose, entitled *The Last Great Disgrace* focused unprecedented attention on the conditions in all institutions and won him a Peabody Award. (Powers, Ron. *The Newscasters: The News Business as Show Business.* Pg. 185, St. Martin's Press, 1977). The original Willowbrook documentary remains available on Rivera's website.

Willowbrook eventually closed in 1987 and remains the best known example of institutional abuse. It also helped to propel a new institution closure movement that continues to this day.

Closure of institutions requires legislative action and a lot of organizing by people with disabilities and their allies. Often the two biggest opponents are the parents who left their children there years ago and want them left alone along with the public employee unions who argue against closure on the basis of job loss and economic hardship to the host communities.

The other method of course is litigation which has been effective but is time consuming, expensive and fraught with peril.

Here in Oregon the closure of Fairview was a combination of interventions by the US Department of Justice, litigation by Disability Rights Oregon and enormous community organizing by advocates. After years of bitter struggle it finally closed on February 24, 2000.

The actual moment one of these closes is highly poignant for the residents, the community and those who witness it. I was on hand the day Fairview closed and wrote a story for the Portland newspaper about it. Witnessing this was a once in a lifetime opportunity and for that reason I am including the article below. It remains one of the few published accounts of the last day of a giant.

"In the end it was just green grass and vast, empty buildings. The mass of humanity going about its business; the smell, the bedlam, the shrieks, the love and the drama of human life are gone. In a moment all that became part of history; a part of our collective memory.

Last Thursday, a small group of staff, state officials and advocates met informally in front of LeBreton Hall on the grounds of the Fairview Training Center. Some stared into space, their minds occupied with memories, some joked, some dabbed at moist eyes, and some took pictures. Over all of us lay the anticipation of a once-unimaginable and long awaited event. It happened, finally, at 1:15 p.m.

A green minivan pulled up in front of LeBreton and stopped. No one seemed to know what to do. A few of us waived to the occupant in the front passenger seat. He smiled and waved back. For him a new life was beginning as another, older and more ordered life came to an end.

The van pulled out and disappeared. Leaving in it was the last, the very last, resident of Fairview Training Center.

In the superintendent's office we examined the entries in the large, musky, leather-bound ledgers, their endless sheets filled with careful renderings, the pages yellow and stiff from age and from the dried ink so painstakingly applied by generations of clerks. On the pages are columns marked "inmates".

Here are the daily counts. "February 24, 1917, 371 inmates." Soon their number would exceed 3,000. The names of the new "inmates" were carefully recorded and each assigned an "inmate number". Also entries such as this: "March 16, 1921, inmate #...died. Remains shipped to family in Cave Junction." The ledgers are an archive not only of an institution but also of the meticulous detail attended to by the keepers of these "inmates."

There are scrapbooks of clippings from newspaper stories. Aging photos of goofy kids dressed up for a parade. Construction of the pond. Later, newsworthy pictures of young people bowling "in the community."

These are also stories of lost "inmates," of fires, murder and death. Images of faces smiling and laughing, a lasting testament to human spirit and resilience. I see that face every morning: My daughter has one just like it.

In 1981 the clippings began to tell another story; one of lawsuits, investigations, charges and counter-charges. That ended on Feb. 24, 2000 at 1:15 p.m. There will be no more clippings.

Slowly we walked around the silent and empty campus with two former "inmates" who remembered their lives at Fairview Training Center. The infirmary where one went for a knee operation only to learn that they had operated on her healthy hip by mistake. Another pointed out the spot where she was run over by a staff vehicle. To save money her knee was fused, rather than repaired. Thirty years later it still will not bend.

We walked into the empty "cottages," now smelling of cleaning products and echoing the sound of our footsteps. "Oh, no, it wasn't like this when I lived here," our commentator said. "Then there were no partitions of any kind. All of us girls slept on cots next to one another. There was never any privacy." She remembered how as a child she was frightened of "the big heads," the ones with hydrocephalus who leaned on the wall and groaned.

Finally, we passed the plaque on the wall of Fairview's first building. It commemorates the names of the superintendent, state officials and architect responsible for completing this project for the "Oregon Home for the Feeble Minded—1919."

We walked back to LeBreton and got into the van. We drove off with one of the former "inmates." She had to return to her full-time job and at the end of the day would go home to her own apartment. There she would be alone with the memories of a life that once labeled her a "victim of..." and an "inmate".

Farewell Fairview Training Center. You were born of a bad idea in 1908. You left us on a brisk and shining afternoon in the midst of an Oregon winter. Rest in Peace.

May your kind never pass our way again."

This article appeared in the Commentary Section of **The Oregonian** newspaper on February 29, 2000.

Attitudes had begun to change when it came to the deficit model of disability. The institution closure movement gained momentum in 2000 when Congress passed a new version of the Developmental Disabilities Act. The language of the act could not be more different than the practice prevalent until then. Although the dream of an institution free US remains elusive Congress has given that dream considerable legal ammunition to achieve that goal. It reads as follows:

"...assure that individuals with developmental disabilities and their families participate in the design of plans to access needed community services, individualized supports and other forms of assistance that promote self-determination, independence, productivity and integration and inclusion in all aspects of community life." (AIDD website, retrieved Sept, 22, 2015).

The pillars of eugenics was sterilization and segregation. Most of the dirty work of eugenics took place within the walls of state sanctioned institutions. The two are linked in perpetuity. After forced sterilization was no longer fashionable the pro institution lobby doubled down on segregation. Their rationale is based on the deficit model of disability long ago discredited by advocates. Institutions are first and foremost rationalized as a 'safe place' for 'those people' to be kept. Out of sight out of mind. While family anxiety about closure and moving to the community is understandable it has also been addressed in a thousand ways. Community living is safe, normal, natural and with proper supports a vastly better place to spend one's life. Why then are they so hard to close?

Institutions have always been defended on the idea that the segregation is for the good of the residents. Advocacy has laid that idea to rest. Modern institutions are scandalously expensive to operate and the money to support one person ($500,000 a biennium in the case of Fairview) can be used to support many in the community. One would expect the cost savings to be appealing to legislators. But like many evils there is always another cover to fall back on. In this case economic wellbeing of the host communities has, in too many cases, taken on the role of apologist for what is clearly segregation.

Institutions are typically staffed by workers from public employee unions particularly the American Federation of State, County and Municipal Employees. (AFSCME). Consistent with the 'out of sight out of mind' philosophy of segregation most institutions are located in rather pastoral settings in small towns. The institution, originally established with the fiction that it was best for the residents, has now become the economic engine that runs the local economies. While it is understandable that these communities are concerned about their economic vitality would it not be better to ask what it says about

Americans with disabilities and just how much they matter?

By rationalizing continued segregation pro institution arguments simply reduce human beings to commodity. It really makes no difference if they are talking about keeping an institution open or an aircraft factory. The fact is that the product generating the money are the lives, freedom, dignity and self-determination of tens of thousands of human lives.

Human lives are not the same as airplane parts. It is the height of moral vacuity to argue otherwise. It was far more honest to believe segregation was the answer than it is to reduce people to a public works project. Union hysteria combined with their legislative power has produced a sort of stalemate. People want out. The union wants them in. And, as is true far more often than it should be, the needs of people take a back seat to the worship of money.

Up until the passage of the Americans with Disabilities Act (ADA) in 1990 there were few legal tools to use to argue for community inclusion and institution closure. The ADA certainly raised the awareness of the public to some of the barriers people with disabilities face. But the actual law addresses things like public space accessibility, new construction, employment discrimination, etc. It says nothing about the right to live in the community like everyone else. That weapon had to wait for the United States Supreme Court.

Two women, Lois Curtis and Elaine Wilson, who have developmental disabilities and mental illness, had been voluntarily admitted to the Georgia Regional Hospital and housed in the psychiatric unit. Following treatment professionals certified both of them ready to be released into the community. Due to capacity issues with community supports Georgia refused to move them and each spent several additional years locked up in an institution. Failing all other relief they filed suit naming the Georgia Department of Human Services and its' administrator Mr. Olmstead as defendants.

On June 22, 1999 the Supreme Court held in *Olmstead v L.C. (527 US 581(1999)* the court held that unjustified segregation of persons with disabilities constitutes discrimination under Title II of the Americans with Disabilities Act. Title II applies to all activities, services and programs of any public entity including, of course, states.

The court held that those public entities must provide community based services to people with disabilities when (1) they are appropriate (2) the affected persons do not oppose community living and (3) community based services can be reasonably accommodated, taking into account the public entities resources and the needs of others receiving services.

The court explained that its holding "reflects two evident judgments." First 'institutional placement of persons who can handle and benefit from community settings perpetuates unwarranted assumptions that persons so isolated are incapable of or unworthy of participating in community life.' Second, 'confinement in an institution severely diminishes the everyday life activities of individuals, including family relations, social contact, work options, economic independence, educational advancement, and culture enrichment.'

Olmstead is even more important in the context of our history. From the beginning we have seen how people with disabilities, women and racial minorities were left out of the founding documents. After centuries of being virtually invisible in the public arena people with disabilities were suddenly not only recognized but declared (with some limitations) worthy of main stream life as a constitutional right. The ruling provided sound legal authority to fight for the deinstitutionalization of people with disabilities and we will later consider specific examples.

The value that drives the deinstitutionalization movement is a long delayed recognition that segregation is wrong. It is wrong applied on the basis of race, education, gender and religion. And it is wrong on the basis of disability. Segregation is the opposite of inclusion. Its' evils have caused more harm than virtually any other nasty habit left over from the white, male, property owner days. When it comes to segregation Dr. Martin Luther King, Jr. said it best.

"All segregation statutes are unjust because segregation distorts the soul and damages the personality. It gives the segregator a false sense of supremacy and the segregated a false sense of inferiority. Segregation, to use the terminology of the Jewish philosopher Martin Buber, substitutes and 'I it' relationship for an 'I thou' relationship and ends up relegating persons to the status of things. Hence, segregation is not only politically, economically, and sociologically unsound, it is morally wrong and sinful." (Quoted from Reider, Jonathan. *Gospel of Freedom: Martin Luther King's Letter from the Birmingham Jail and the Struggle that Changed a Nation.* Westchester. 2014).

After centuries of 'care' and virtual house arrest people with disabilities began to take matters into their own hands. Paul Longmore wrote at length about disabled versus non-disabled interest. By that he meant not only those whose interests were openly hostile but also about those who imagine themselves allies but in fact co-opt every initiative to their own advantage be it running non-profits, staffing agencies or speaking on behalf of people with disabilities. He points out that regardless of good intentions there is no authentic voice unless it comes from a person with a disability. (Longmore, pp 131-138).

There are a number of reasons given for this change from passivity to self-advocacy and a notion of disability power. Things like cross disability agendas, coalitions and mutual respect were still a bit in the future but the fact remains that people with disabilities began to assert themselves in ways the nation had not seen.

One reason for this change is the parents' movement of the 1950s. Coalescing primarily around education parents began to question why their disabled children were not able to attend school. That agitation led to the founding of national organizations focused on educational reform. By 1974 the earliest version of what would come to be known as the Individuals with Disabilities Education Act (IDEA). From 1974 all children in the United States enjoyed the right to a free and appropriate public education. Implementation has been an issue but strategically the picture changed dramatically once schools were required to accept and educate all children. A revolution of rising expectations if ever there was one. This success grew with the rising sense of solidarity and purpose. The social isolation of children and their care giver parents had ended and other groups learned from the experience.

Let us be clear. IDEA was not the result of people with disabilities asserting themselves. Families did that. Likewise the Association of Retarded Citizens would have been more accurately called the Association of Retarded Citizens Mommies. (Today the Arc has dropped the r word and, increasingly progressive and responsive to disabled voices, plays a big role in shaping national policy. Its' effectiveness did not end by changing with the times.) But factors other than the parent movement were also afoot to change the landscape and help launch real disability power.

One factor was the establishment of a national vocational rehabilitation (VR) program whose mission was to find work for World War II veterans who had been disabled during the war. The stated purpose was to return them to work where they could be financially self-supporting and contribute to the culture as a whole. The idea that an investment of public money now would result in integrated independent living was a new one and set the stage for a lot that followed.

Although the inclusion of people with physical, intellectual and developmental disabilities in the VR scheme was still decades in the future it did provide a window on what might be possible. Today employment of people with disabilities (and how they are employed) is very much a front burner issue as we shall see. But the movement began with the example of VR.

At about the same time as VR improvements in medical care, particularly the use of antibiotics and increased awareness of nutrition, meant that people with disabilities lived much longer. When my daughter was born in 1988 medical experts told us she had a life expectancy of about sixteen years. Their data was not wrong. It was just based on institutionalize people with Down syndrome dying of asphyxia pneumonia from gobbling oatmeal from the wooden spoons held in front of them by staff. The death rate had to do with abuse. It had nothing to do with Down syndrome.

For politicians concerned about government programs the sudden longevity of people with disabilities meant that expensive institutional confinement would continue to increase in cost. That fear of increased cost at last began to cause state legislatures to consider the possibility of moving people into independent community living as a way to control cost. The effort to close the institution here in Oregon informative.

At legislative 'coffees' in homes every candidate was invited to spend an evening with a person or family who had experienced or were in danger of institutionalization. The short version is that democrats were appalled at the civil rights issues and jumped on board. A lot of them jumped right off when the figured out that the staff were union members who opposed closure. The republicans didn't seem to care much about the segregation one way or the other but the $500,000 per biennium cost got their attention and when the vote for closure neared they were far less wavering then their democratic colleagues. The economic argument proved more reliable than the civil liberty one

In the late 1940s and early 1950s there was a resurgence of interest among academics in the 'fields' of mental illness and mental retardation. A consensus arose, not unlike the one rationalizing eugenics as sound science, that mental illness was an adult issue while mental retardation was seen as an issue of childhood. In 1950 Pearl Buck wrote a popular novel about her own child entitled "The Child Who Never Grew Up." Depictions of people in institutions related how both men and women were clothed and treated like young children. This thinking gave rise to the notion of mental age. Namely that a person with a chronological age of thirty two and a mental age of six would *be*—i.e. would act like—a child of six years. That diagnosis, albeit somewhat changed in its modern form, is with us to this day. (See Dybwad, Gunnar. "Setting the Stage Historically" in *New Voices: Self-Advocacy by People with Disabilties.* Dybwad, Gunnar and Bersani, Hank. Editors. Brookline, 1995.)

This sense of disability as perpetual childhood was given emphasis in 1960 when an influential 'professional' conference was held in Boston and entitled *Outlook for the Adult Retarded*. In a presentation on "Developing Patterns of Aid to the Aging Retarded and their Families." For the first time attention was called to the lengthening life spans of persons identified as being mentally retarded and raised the obvious problem of a proper home for such people. Although some participants spoke of a preference for solving that problem in the community the majority saw no option but more and bigger institutions. There is no evidence that anyone with a disability was asked what they thought. (Dybwad)

Indeed at this stage of our story there is little evidence at all that people with disabilities, especially intellectual and developmental disabilities, were ever considered fellow persons deserving of respect or consideration. With the dawning of the diagnostic era the circle had pretty much closed around them. Pity followed by fear and segregation. Medical experiments, eugenics, evaluation, infantilism and exile to the furthest margins of society. This is a good time to make the point that good intentions are not an excuse. The 'science' of disability has proven over and over to be wrong and even deadly. Looking back on the 'best practice' standards and accepted 'fact' of those eras they resemble nothing so much as a dusty and dry Baroque exhibit in a tasteless and out-of-the way museum. How could educated people have ever believed such things?

Just who were these disabled people? These mostly invisible and shunned people? About them there are some things we know for certain. The first is that they were here. Disability is a normal and natural part of the human condition and has been with us from the very beginning. But what were their lives like? We know from Herodotus and Thucydides that the Spartans took disabled babies and put them to death and we know from Shakespeare that there were court jesters: objects of both mirth and abhorrence. As to the feeling, hungering, longing, wistful, lonely and inevitably short lives of those millions we know virtually nothing. History is blank when it comes to finding even one individual with an intellectual or developmental disability whose existence is remembered. There are no positive role models. All of the hopes and dreams of this giant multitude of humans is lost. Overwhelmed by blackness and eternal night because no cared enough to write their story.

That is the great sadness.

Non-disabled interests in the form of reformers, clergy, 'scientists', busy bodies, and politicians had all combined to control the lives of Americans with disabilities. The foundations of the disability industrial complex in which people with disabilities themselves were limited to one role; providing the fuel to make the monster go, was upon us. And as that monster grew billions of dollars found their way into the pockets of those who ran it, worked within it and enabled it. Everyone had a vested interest in keeping things just as they were. Non-disabled interests had institutionalized the medical/deficit model. The result was disability being seen as a social problem that required policy makers and professionals attention while simultaneously (and tragically) depoliticizing it by placing it under the authority of medical and quasi-medical interests. By casting disability as a pathology the medical model had reduced it to a purely individualized and personal condition. Rather like having a cold. Personal conditions defy systematic study. For United States citizens with disabilities to break out of that mold required something quite revolutionary, threatening and unexpected. It required a disability rights movement.

A disabled interest is one identified by people with disabilities themselves. The community organizing, action strategy and implementation are all carried out by people with disabilities for people with disabilities. Non-disabled allies may be an integral part of the movement but they are not in charge. Where were the non-disabled interests?

In 1935 the great depression was in full swing. Protests were common but the one that began on May 29 was different than any that had been seen before. Six young adults—three women and three men—entered the office of the Emergency Relief Bureau in New York City. They demanded to see the director and when told he would not be available until the next week vowed that they would stay 'until hell freezes over.'

What was different about those six people and their supporting picketers were all people with physical disabilities. All were seeking employment and claimed discrimination against people with disabilities by the Works Progress Administration (WPA) a New Deal program for job creation and hiring. Their protest marked the first day of what would come to be known as the League of the Physically Handicapped. During the following several years this militant league fought job discrimination and of equal importance challenged for the first time the deficit model ideology of the early twentieth-century. As time passed they directed their ire and political demands beyond employment and challenged public policies, professional practice and even societal arrangements such as lack of accessibility and educational opportunity. (Longmore, Paul. "The League of the Physically Handicapped and the Great Depression" in *Why I Burned My Book and Other Essays on Disability.* Temple University. 2003.)

After three weeks of protest the group decided to organize formally. In November, 1935 they returned to the WPA and conducted a three week long picketing and demands that the WPA, created to help people find jobs in the private sector stop labeling them "unemployable." A year after their first action members traveled to Washington, DC to meet with WPA boss Harry Hopkins. After the usual stall they eventually did meet with Hopkins who told them he did not believe there were as many disabled job seekers as the League contended and that he would take no action until they convinced him otherwise. After several months of work the League presented Hopkins with a ten page document entitled "Thesis on Conditions of Physically Handicapped." The written demands became common in the years that followed but the League is remembered as the first to put demands directly into the face of a government leader. They described discrimination in both the public and private sectors and recommended preferential hiring of disabled veterans and civilians with physical disabilities and criticized vocational rehabilitation programs as being underfunded and inadequate. Forecasting later struggles they also objected to being sent to job sites as strike breakers.

In September of 1936, in its most revolutionary act, the League joined forces with The League for the Advancement of the Deaf and gave birth to cross disability advocacy that would prove both illusive and the key to success in future actions. Mostly their demands were ignored and the few people hired were laid off a few months later. But the demands they made addressed issues that would later dominate the 1970s and 1980s. Significantly their direct action tactics of sit-ins, picketing and confrontational politics is similar to what ADAPT would use in the future. Finally, and perhaps most important, the League openly attacked the deficit model of disability and instead offered up evidence of the societal barriers plaguing people with disabilities. (Brown, Stephen. *The League of the Physically Handicapped and Independent Living in 1935.* Houston, 2000. Retrieved from the internet 10/5/15.

League picket signs read "We Do Not Want Tin Cups" and "We Want Jobs." As professor Brown wrote "The first could be used to predate the current movement against telethons and the second to protest... The current unemployment rate among people with disabilities."

The League established a base for future activism. The spark was lit but many years would pass before it burst into flame and changed the landscapes of life for people with disabilities.

Although the League failed to establish a lasting disability power movement it did set a powerful example that may have left the service system unmoved but began to cause individuals and small, informal groups of individuals to begin to think differently. Change did not come from the top. Change came slowly and it gravitated from the aspirations of isolated men and women who first questioned the circumstance of their own lives and began to draw connections with others. Who all these people were is, like so much disability history, lost. But they were born, lived and died. Often in anonymity. But it was their spark that lit the fire that became the disability rights movement.

One of these people is Gini Laurie. Born in St. Louis in 1913 she was named Virginia Grace Wilson. The child of a physician who had treated patients during the great polio epidemic of 1912 she was named Virginia in honor of one of her two sisters who had perished in the outbreak. Polio defined to large degree her future work but she also became one of the first advocates to create and support the idea of cross disability coalitions.

After graduation from college she hoped to become a physician but finding gender based obstacles at every turn settled on secretarial training and began volunteer work with the American Red Cross. Her husband, Joseph Laurie, served in the army during World War II and the couple traveled a great deal eventually settling in Cleveland, Ohio. Her volunteer work during the polio epidemic of 1949 brought her into contact with many survivors, their families and volunteer support people.

At the time polio survivors were often hospitalized for many months or even years. Their only contact was with medical staff, volunteer support people and each other. Naturally they developed close friendships with fellow patients. These bonds were broken when one of them was finally discharged. No mechanisms existed for keeping in touch and any sense of community ended with the discharge. Laurie would later comment that it "was apparent that what polio survivors had two vital needs...people and information. They wanted to keep up with each other...and wanted to share information about their lives and equipment." (Laurie, Gini, et al. *Handbook on the Late Effects of Poliomyelitis for Physicians and Survivors.* St. Louis. 1984).

She and her husband established a newsletter for polio survivors that kept relationships alive and empowered individuals to learn about others and eventually to begin questioning why it was so hard to live independently in the community. At first her newsletter focused primarily on maintaining the bonds polio survivors had already established with each other. But its mission quickly expanded. Higher education was a concern and she began publishing articles written by people with disabilities on their experiences attempting to finish their educations. She was among the first to identify attendant care, transportation, employment and travel. She concluded that the best way to combat the persistent barriers was to publicize the successes of people in the community. This new direction for the newsletter naturally broadened into other disabilities and stories of success or at least attempts to lead a normal life.

As a result she became a loud and early critic of institutions and exposing them as unnecessarily expensive alternatives to community living. Until her death she agitated for professional attendant care. As early as 1963 she began publishing articles on what would come to be known as the independent living philosophy. Although she herself referred to it as interdependent living as a descriptor of human lives disabled or not. (Laurie).

Her magazine supported the forming of the American Coalition of Citizens with Disabilities, a civil rights organization created, administered and lead by people with disabilities. She was the only member of the board of directors without a disability. Her work helping disabled residents move from nursing homes and other institutions into the community helped form the first small groups of what became to be known as Centers for Independent Living. Today there are more than 600 of them. Each run, managed and staffed by a majority of employees with disabilities.

Incrementally Laurie helped to create a vision of equality and community living that is at the root of the modern independent living movement. She is far from the only person who questioned the status quo during those years but she is one we know and remember. She and her known and unknown associates laid the foundation for the assertion of disability power that was about to break over the American landscape.

Up until now people like Gini Laurie (who would today be regarded as a non-disabled ally) from time to time did remarkable things what was lacking was major political muscle being shown by people with disabilities themselves. Social isolation, hopelessness, poverty, health issues and other factors all contributed their malignant influence on disability organizing and assertion of disabled interests. All of that was about to change forever with the passage of Section 504 of the Rehabilitation Act and the fight over its implementing regulations. The world of disability politics would never be the same.

The Civil Rights Act of 1964 glaringly did not include any mention of disability. Disappointed advocates and Congressional allies sought to add disability protection to some other legislative vehicle and in 1973 they did so by adding language from Title VI of the Civil Rights Act to the final draft of the Rehabilitation Act. For the first time federal law promised civil rights for persons with a disability. This new provision (twice vetoed by Richard Nixon) became section 504.

"No otherwise qualified individual with a disability in the United States,...shall solely by reason of his or her disability, be excluded from participation in, be denied the benefits of, or be subjected to discrimination under any program or activity receiving Federal financial assistance or under any program or activity conducted by any Executive agency or by the United States Postal Service."

29 USC 794.

In the late 1960s a severely disabled man named James Cherry enrolled at Howard University Law School. Howard, of course, is a traditionally Afro-American institution and Cherry soon noted the similarities between the fledgling civil rights movement and the plight of Americans with disabilities. To assure his access to the law school instruction Cherry petitioned the administration for a designated parking space nearby and requested a key to the service elevator in order to get to class. The school's administrators did not agree and denied Cherry's requests.

Following passage of section 504 in 1973 Cherry began writing to the Department of Health, Education and Welfare (HEW) to ask them to issue 504 regulations so that he might again make his case. This time with the backing of federal legislation. Ultimately he filed a law suit against HEW secretary David Mathews and in 1976 the court ruled in Cherry's favor. By them Jimmy Carter had been elected president and Joseph Califano was the new secretary of HEW.

During his campaign Carter had promised to listen to disabled people and aid them in their fight for equal rights. Reasonable the community expected more of him than the Nixon Administration. Fearing that the new administration was not moving fast enough to get the 504 regulations issued the disability community met with Califano. Sensing delay they threatened direct action of regulations were not issued quickly.

On April 5, 1977 negotiations with Califano broke down. Immediately the disability community staged demonstrations and sit-ins at all of the HEW regional offices. Notably the one in San Francisco lasted for twenty-five days and involved participation by activists from all over the country. The sidewalks around the building were full of supporters, police effort to try to clear the building were thwarted by political organizing and protest and national media began covering the protesters. All to the great embarrassment of Califano and the Carter administration. At last, on April 28, 1977

Califano signed the regulations and, significantly, did the same with the implementing regulations for the Education for All Handicapped Children Act. The fight over 504 had, for the first time, united disability activists into a cohesive national movement. Disability power had arrived. And the fledgling new movement looked ahead eagerly for more opportunity to assert its interests free of careerists, bureaucrats and assorted disability parasites who had so long controlled policy. The country would never again be the same. (See Floyd, Barbara L. (editor) *From Institutions to Independence: A History of People with Disabilities in Northwest Ohio.* University of Toledo. 2010).

The 504 direct action showed that disability power was possible. For the first time people could see that community organizing was key to turning the medical/deficit model of disability on its head. This was achieved by people with disabilities leading, organizing and putting their bodies and comfort on the line to achieve a result non-disabled 'leaders' and interests had written off as impossible. At about the same time other rumblings of disability power took root.

In 1971 a minister and civil rights worked named Wade Blank was hired by a provider agency in Denver called Heritage House. The night before beginning his new job Blank visited the facility and recorded "The place was like a morgue. The food was cold." Blank was shocked when on the first day of work he saw sixty young people leaving at 7:30 in the morning to go to a workshop where they spent the day counting fish hooks. His introduction to a sub minimum wage work activities program.

The next three years were an awakening for Blank. He listened to the residents and took steps to implement their wishes. "I allowed them to evaluate staff. They wanted co-ed living. They wanted to have pets. They wanted to have rock and roll bands. Three years in I was trying to change it from inside, and I didn't understand the monster I worked for," he recalled. (Retrieved from ADAPT website, Oct. 19, 2015.)

In a classic example of disabled versus non-disabled interests Blank proposed moving people out of the Heritage House nursing home and into apartments of their own where services would follow them. For that effort he was promptly fired. "They came in and they took all the stereos and TVs our of everybody's rooms, had the dog pound come by and get all the animals and in one day it went from everything I'd built for four years—to that." Undeterred he vowed that he would do it himself.

Over the next six months he had moved eighteen 'severely' disabled people out of the nursing home and into apartments of their own. This exodus lead to the founding of the Atlantis Community in Denver and its political-direct-action off shoot ADAPT. (The acronym then stood for American Disabled for Accessible Public Transportation)

At the time interstate buses were not required to provide accessibility for people in wheelchairs. If you could not walk up the entry steps you simply could not ride. ADAPT took on this discrimination first in Denver's and then the nation's bus systems. Using direct action tactics similar to those perfected by Dr. King's movement ADAPTers blockaded buses, clogged depots, made bold demands and achieved extraordinary results.

Blank was among the first to very clearly state the connection between the civil rights movement and the disability rights movement. "All the issues were the same. The black movement wanted to ride buses equally. The black movement wanted to eat at Woolworth's counters. The black movement wanted the right to vote. The black movement wanted the right to keep their families together. The black movement wanted the right to be integrated into the school system. That is what the disability rights movement wants—exactly." (ADAPT web page).

"So I said (Blank explained) let's take 25 wheelchairs and go out and surround a bus and hold it and see what happens. Like magic it worked. Total power. Police couldn't move the wheelchairs because they were afraid. The mayor said 'don't arrest disabled people. We win." (Johnson, Mary and Shaw, Barrett. *To Ride the Public's Buses: The Fight that Built a Movement.* Advocado Press (2001).

From the beginning in Denver ADAPT turned its attention to community living and the crippling effect of the Medicaid 'institutional bias.' Medicaid was created as a federal funding mechanism to help 'licensed facilities'. License facilities meaning congregate settings like giant institutions and nursing homes. These are the very things people with disabilities do not want.

As a follow up to the transportation success ADAPT made community supports for people with disabilities its major issue. Many ADAPT members had themselves only recently been liberated from one institutional setting or another. Their desire to help others do the same lead to MiCASSA (Medicaid Community Attendant Services and Supports Act) a proposed legislation that if enacted would allow people with disabilities on Medicaid to choose whether to spend money on nursing homes or on personal care attendants. ADAPT pointed out that community care is far cheaper than institutional care. In a classic confrontation between disabled and non-disabled interests ADAPT pitted itself against the powerful nursing home lobby and its Congressional power. That fight continues but significant changes have occurred in the law of Medicaid waiver and today more people than ever are living in their own homes with appropriate and self-directed supports.

Today there are more than thirty ADAPT chapters scattered around the country. Lead by people with all kinds of disabilities it is now the leading edge of the disability rights movement. Each year at least two direct actions (meaning civil disobedience and arrest) occur. With the passage of the Affordable Care Act ADAPT has turned its considerate muscle against states that have turned down a provision called the Community Choice Option. That provision provides states with huge financial incentives to support independent community living. Today the quality of life and independence of people in states that have adopted it are dramatically different and better than the ones that have not. This of course is another example of state's rights which we talked so much about in Part 1. In the 1960s states were able to mask their racism by hiding behind their claim of state's rights. Today many of those same states hide their prejudice and ableism behind the same mantra. Their real message also has racist overtones. Hatred of President Obama outweighs the quality of life of their disabled citizens. And that struggle continues.

Perhaps the most radical step taken by ADAPT has been its willingness to take on not only the economic hierarchy of the disability industrial complex but also a disability hierarchy that for too long separated people based on labels. Disability power is cross disability power. Again Blank said it best "You go around to independent living centers and you'll see a lot of post polios and a lot of spinal cord injuries. But you don't see people who slobber or can't speak clearly." He condemned the more 'respectable' disability organizations and their disability pecking orders.

Another revolutionary change ADAPT can take credit for is the empowerment of people with disabilities themselves. It has made it possible for people who had never before thought it possible to be leaders: people labeled mentally retarded and others typically disenfranchised both by society at large and by traditional disability organizations. Blank had no patience for people who put their own egos or their own careers above the needs of the movement. Today there are hundreds of independent living centers scattered across every state and territory. By law a majority of staff and board must be made up on people with disabilities themselves. Taken together they exert enough collective power in a disabled interest way to counter the provider and workshop lobby so well-funded by its non-disabled interest agenda.

The impact of ADAPT cannot be measured simply by legislative or administrative victories but more importantly be the impact it has on its own members and supporters. Over the past thirty years thousands of people have participated in direct action with ADAPT. Many have gone to jail. The experience has changed all of their lives. Far from learned passivity ADAPT demonstrates the people united can never be defeated. It is a formidable force.

One ADAPT activist described their first action to me. "I couldn't believe it. All the decisions were made by people like me. People with pretty involved disabilities. What I saw were people with disabilities taking care of other people with disabilities. Having sex with other people with disabilities. Going to jail, singing, laughing and crying together. Everything was captioned. Support needs were met by us without agencies or bosses or anyone telling us what to do. When it ended I got up on the speakers at the last night party and danced. I haven't missed one since."

Wade Blank was a minister by trade and was not a person with a disability. What radicalized him to direct action and confrontational politics? Interesting to note his reaction to his first day at Heritage House. The first was the cold food. The other was his amazement that people could be hauled off every morning in a bus to go to 'work' counting fishhooks for pennies an hour. His reaction is not a surprise nor is it uncommon. Most Americans have no idea the their countrymen and women with intellectual and developmental disabilities are exempt from minimum wage laws and can be paid nothing or nearly nothing for their labor. And they can be forgiven for wondering why this is called 'employment' and how it could be true.

The origin of sub minimum wage can be traced back to our discussion of the Perkins Institute for the Blind. In 1840 it introduced employment that was 'sheltered' from competition in order to create jobs. That notion may have been state of the art in 1840. Now, going on two centuries later it is a quaint notion. But it is also the law of the United States.

In 1935 President Franklin D. Roosevelt approved the practice by Executive Order. In 1938 it was codified into law as part of the Fair Labor Standards Act. It created a special exemption (now referred to as section 14(c), that allowed employers to pay workers with disabilities less than minimum wage. This was rationalized as a way to rehabilitate workers for a 'reasonable' time in order to train them for competitive employment. (William, Whittaker, *Treatment of Workers with Disabilities Under Section 14(c) of the Fair Labor Standards Act*. Federal Publications #209. 2005). Over the years reasonable came to mean never. Once a person enters one of these places they can be there for decades. And thousands are.

Today the Department of Labor Wage and Hour Division certifies employers, allowing them to pay less than prevailing wage to a worker if their disability is found to interfere with productivity. This method of sheltered employment gained popularity during the 1950s and 1960s and continued far beyond the adoption of the 1963 Developmental Disabilities Assistance Act and Bill of Rights (often called the DD Act) called for support and opportunities that promote independence, productivity and inclusion of people with disabilities in the community.

Goodwill Industries is the most commonly known of these providers. Claiming that paying a competitive wage would put them out of business they consistently advertise lavishly, pay their executives outrageous salaries (In 2013 the one in Oregon was paid $800,000) and have lobbyists on site in Washington, DC to protect the golden calf. One can see why. A business model in which inventory is donated and workers not paid a living wage really can't fail. Unless one regards the dependency and degradation of the workers as a failure. Which, of course, the country does not.

By the 1970s sheltered workshops were the norm and a highly profitable one at that. To justify the practice the Department of Health, Education and Welfare from time to time contracted with private firms to 'report on and analyze' the practice. Reviewing these reports now what one sees are massive numbers of charts, percentages, absentee rates, and enrollment etc. all expensively and carefully presented in a way to justify and practice. An example is a 467 page tome entitled *The Role of the Sheltered Workshops in the Rehabilitation of the Severely Handicapped*. Greenleigh and Assoc. Inc., New York. 1977. The reports concludes that "workshops yield a positive benefit to society for money invested. (Page 343).

All of the analysis is from the perspective of employers making money while doing good charitable deeds. No thought is given to the need for disabled people to earn a living wage, experience dignity or become assimilated members of the American mainstream. The wants and the needs of the workers themselves were simply not considered worthy of mention.

All of this rather floated along unchallenged and unquestioned until January, 2011 when the National Disability Rights Network (NDRN) issued is ground breaking report entitled *Segregated and Exploited: The Failure of the Disability Service System to Provide Quality Work*. Executive Director Curt Decker began the report with a "letter from the Executive Director." It is worth quoting in part.

'Dear Friends,

Today, across the United States of America, hundreds of thousands of people with disabilities are being isolated and financially exploited by their employers. Many are segregated away from traditional work and kept out of sight. Most are paid only a fraction of the minimum wage while many company owners make six-figure salaries. Many people profit off of their labor. All, except the worker. For many people with disabilities, their dream of leaving their 'job training program' will never come true. They labor away making only a tiny portion of what they should because there is a system in place that provides no true alternatives.

...

Unfortunately, sheltered workshops and the subminimum wage still exist today because of self-interested employers and systematic neglect by the federal agencies, buttressed by out dated stereotypes of people with disabilities and the low expectations held by the general public, lawmakers, and, sadly, even some families and the disability community. Simply put, sheltered workshops are just another institution segregating people with disabilities away because of our unwillingness to accept that our perceived notions about their ability to work may be wrong.

This call to action is long overdue. It is time to end segregated work, sheltered employment and sub-minimum wage. Now."

The report continued with three very specific recommendations.

1. *End Segregated Employment and Sub-minimum wage for people with disabilities.*
   a. Restrict all federal and state money that is spent on employers who segregate employees with disabilities from the general workforce.
   b. End the ability of employers to pay employees with disabilities a sub-minimum wage.
   c. End all programs that emphasize moving young adults from the classroom to a segregated or sub-minimum wage employment environment.

2. *Promote and Facilitate Integrated and Comparable Wage Employment Alternatives.*
   a. Strengthen existing and create new federal and state tax incentives for employers to place people with disabilities in integrated environments with comparable wages.
   b. Assist employees to disabilities to find employment in the general workforce in jobs that they choose.

3. *Increase Labor Protections and Enforcement.*
   a. Fully investigate violations and abuses perpetrated by employers that pay less than minimum wage or segregate workers with disabilities.
   b. Increase penalties for violators.

   c. Formalize standards for employee evaluations and productivity measurements.

   On the morning the report was released the provider community responded quickly and rather hysterically. NDRN was accused of insulting the 'fine men and women' who run sheltered work programs, abandoning 'community solidarity' and generally betraying the good old boy system of 'services.' Rather a long morning for people on the receiving end of the vitriol.

   That all turned around when a large bouquet of flowers arrived. The attached card had an inscription that set the standard for disabled interest vs. non-disabled interest advocacy. It read "Thank you for telling the truth about sheltered workshops." The card was signed "Self-Advocates Becoming Empowered." That was an important moment. The largest cross disability advocacy organization in the world taking leadership from the demands of people with intellectual and developmental disabilities signaled a new partnership of equals together addressing real issues and with mutual respect.

   In April, 2012 NDRN issued a follow up report entitled *Beyond Segregated and Exploited: Update on the Employment of People with Disabilities."* Although repeal of 14(c) requires Congressional action which in turn means a functional Congress (something the USA currently lacks) advocates were never the less able to accomplish a great deal. Perhaps the most important of which was moving sheltered employment out of the category on dirty little secret and into the light of day.

   Kansas became the first state to adopt an "Employment First" statute requiring state agencies to develop a plan to place people with disabilities in competitive and integrated settings. Florida, Utah and Alaska launched efforts to assure their states were properly implementing protections for workshop employees. Initiatives to educate people with disabilities of their employment options began in the District of Columbia, Washington, Louisiana, Maine, Ohio and West Virginia. Other states introduced legislation to prevent state contracts from going to sheltered workshops. In all states the question of sub minimum wage employment became a front and center issue generally pitting people with disabilities and their allies against the non-disabled interests of for profit providers. A very healthy exchange.

Perhaps the most serious challenge to the *status quo* came in Oregon. On January 12, 2012 Disability Rights Oregon (joined by two *pro bono* law firms and later the Civil Rights Division of the Department of Justice) filed a lawsuit alleging that the state failed to provide supported employment services in the most integrated setting as required by *Olmstead*. In an historic ruling the court in Portland held that the community integration mandate of *Olmstead* combined with the least restrictive environment provisions of the ADA could result in people with disabilities actually having the right to leave sheltered employment and require states to provide appropriate supports to make that happen.

In 2015 the case settled favorably to the plaintiffs. Oregon agreed to stop sending young adults from transition into segregated employment and adopted a firm time table for the end of sheltered workshops.

It is important for advocates to know and share the fact that anyone can work at a productive job given the proper supports. Sheltered employment is still with us and has powerful lobbyists and consortiums to defend it in Congress. But its' time is passed. In another decade or two my prediction is that it will join eugenics and institutional care on the dust bin of disability history. And, by the way, if anyone challenges you on the reality of integrated employment ask them if they have ever heard of Stephen Hawking.

Nothing has insulted the integrity of people with disabilities more than the medical profession. In 2006 a hospital in Seattle, Washington performed surgery on a child with disabilities by using high doses of estrogen, a hysterectomy, breast bud removal and appendectomy to assure this person would remain forever in a child's body thus making the parents care less burdensome. The procedure quickly became known as the "Ashley treatment.' Adding insult to injury people with disabilities who are not considered important enough to be on organ transplant lists learned that the costs of the surgery were fully covered by the family insurance.

Reaction was swift and furious. As expected the non-disabled interests lashed back defending the family and their wishes. What they missed of course is the obvious question. No one asked Ashley.

In his letter introducing a new NDRN report, *Devaluing People With Disabilities: Medical Procedures that Violate Civil Rights,* Executive Director Curt Decker wrote "... the Ashley Treatment...is the latest and most disgraceful point on the long continuum of ways our society devalues and violates the rights of people with disabilities."

Of a jury verdict in Oregon that awarded a couple $3 million for the 'wrongful birth' of their child Decker wrote "In my thirty years as a disability rights attorney and advocate, I often think that I have seen every type of discrimination and harm inflicted on people with disabilities. Unfortunately, humanity still finds ways to surprise and shock even me."

Although the hospital in Seattle agreed, under pressure, not to perform this procedure again the American Medical Association has refused to condemn or ban it. It is hard to imagine a better example of disabled interests vs.

non-disabled interests than the Ashley treatment. What are the rights of parents? Do they include the right to mutilate their child in the hope of creating a perpetual 'pillow angel?' Does the child have the right to some kind of guardian or advocate to speak for them?

Disability Rights Washington convened a series of conversations with disabled women who came together to talk about their own childhoods, their longing for a baby if they chose, the barriers, the insults and the dehumanizing attitude of society. Those comments are outside the scope of this book but make very compelling reading and can be found in the NDRN report.

Perhaps the most heartening reaction to the Ashley treatment came not from lawyers or agencies but from women with disabilities themselves. ADAPT and the anti-euthanasia group Not Dear Yet joined forces with the Chicago based group FRIDA (Feminist Response in Disability Activism) to take direct action. ADAPT's youth advocates issued a statement in which they "expressed shock and outrage on behalf of the entire national membership of ADAPT."

FRIDA built on ADAPT's statement to organize a direct action campaign against the American Medical Association (AMA), demanding a meeting with AMA membership leadership to discuss the ableism inherent in the Ashley treatment. FRIDA saw the focus on Ashley's female-identified body parts as a devaluing of women with disabilities. Thwarted in their request for a meeting they occupied the AMA headquarters in Chicago. Only after direct action in their own headquarter did the AMA agree to a dialogue.

There are unresolved issues remaining with the Ashley treatment. But the milestone in the history of disability empowerment is the ferocious reaction of people with disabilities speaking on their own behalf and taking direct action without 'advisors', etc. The AMA takeover was notice that the disability rights movement was here and that the days of passive acceptance and silence were forever part of the past. "Nothing About Me Without Me" became more than a slogan. It was a notice. Disability power had arrived.

<u>SELF-ADVOCATES BECOMING EMPOWERED (SABE) AND THE RISE OF SELF-ADVOCACY.</u>

Every individual with a disability suffered at the hands of the medical/deficit model of disability. None more that people with intellectual disabilities. Who would speak for them? Who would understand the plight? Who would combat it?

To the astonishment of the world of professional disability 'leaders' and 'experts' the answer was revolutionary. People with intellectual disabilities would learn to speak for themselves. Turning the tyranny of low expectations on its head a new and powerful voice came of age on the national stage. The age of people with intellectual disabilities providing their own leadership and direction changed everything. A remaining challenge is for policy makers and even some other disability groups to learn to take leadership from self-advocates. Not as some kind of watered down side show. But as a real and powerful new voice. One born of suffering, nurtured on hope and growing in stature every day.

My own introduction to the power of self-advocacy was both dramatic and searing.

To an organization meeting of advisors and self-advocates in Oregon I invited Nancy Ward, later President of Self Advocates Becoming Empowered, to help me facilitate it. At the appointed time I welcomed everyone and introduced Nancy who, in her unassuming way, said the most surprising thing. "All those without disabilities please leave."

At the time it was accepted that advisors would do most of the talking and in the end any plan agreed on would in reality be theirs. They were not happy at being asked to leave. I was thrilled. All day we loafed around the hotel until in late afternoon we were invited back. When we were the plan for self-advocacy in Oregon was announced to us.

I remember thinking "wow. This is how it's done." Nothing about us without us was drilled into my brain long before I had ever heard the phrase.

The origin of the term self-advocate is unclear. My opinion is that when people with disabilities began to speak for themselves that phenomena was so new that it required its own label. Over time it has gone from being revolutionary, to cute, to expected and finally to real power. Today decisions taken without the voices of those affected are bogus by consensus. Some great organizing and politics went into that change. The story of how that came about is instructive.

Valerie Schaaf, herself a person raised in a huge institution, related the origins of in her recollection of meetings in Oregon.

"People First was started in 1973, by those of us who were former residents of Fairview. Our advisor,…took a group of us with him to Vancouver, BC, to a convention for people with disabilities. At the time, individuals up there who were disabled did not speak for themselves; their advisor did all the talking for them, or else the advisors wrote down what they wanted certain individuals to say to those in the audience. The group came back and told us what they saw and heard there. The news from that conference made us feel as though we were a toy or a robot run by remote control. We realized that if we were to continue in this way, we would not be able to have any freedom to live our own lives; we would be like slaves.

This is why People First was born. We wanted to let those in authority know that we were just like them and would like to be treated in the same way. How would you like it if someone did all your talking for you? We wanted to speak for ourselves." (Dybwad, Gunnar & Bersani, Hank, Jr. *New Voices: Self-Advocacy for People with Disabilities.* Brookline. 1996. Page 171).

Had I been more sophisticated at the time of the Oregon meeting I would not have been as surprised at the advisors sense of a proprietary interest in 'their self-advocates.' As we have seen some of the most inhumane and destructive things done to people with disabilities are the result of bright ideas by well-meaning but non-disabled interests. Those advisors were simply reflecting what they had seen and how they had been trained.

Robert Perske, journalist and chronicler of people with intellectual disabilities being executed in the United States, wrote his memories of just how providers, advisors and bureaucrats were trained and conditioned to interact with 'their' disabled people.

"I remember working in institutions in the latter 1950s and 1960s," Perske wrote. "Long before advocacy became a fact. The tasks of a good worker were clear and without equivocation."

*A good worker became the unquestioned mouthpiece for his or her "patients." (We speak for those who cannot speak for themselves.).

- A good worker made oft-repeated use of a single adjective, *appropriate.*
- ("Joe, it's not appropriate for you to speak now," or "Sally, your behavior is inappropriate.
- A good worker hewed to the common denominator. ("Bill, if I let you have this special privilege, then everyone in the ward will want one too.").
- A good worker utilized a herd mentality. ("C'mon gang. Let's head'em up and move 'em out. We have five minutes to get to the dining hall.")
- A good worker knew how to force the right choice. ("James, if you straighten out you can stay in the day room. If you don't, we'll put you in the seclusion room. It's up to you.")
- A good worker offered a paved, one-way street called *benevolence.* ("We must always give to you, but we refuse to let you give to us.").

Perske's memory of institutional life continues in his chilling account of the culture of support workers. He wrote...

- Don't picture it, but try to think about males who were castrated when they began to masturbate. Think about females being sterilized shortly after menstruation.
- "I remember the days when we only needed two drugs," one veteran staff member said. "If someone got too high we knocked them out with chloral hydrate. If they got too depressed we cleaned them out with Epsom salts. It was those conscience objectors during WW II who really messed things up. They were too soft. They could never really control people the way we did."

(Dybwad/Bersani. Pages 19, 20).

Obviously the first step in creating an organization true to the desires and direction of people with disabilities themselves required breaking this perverse relationship between people and their keepers. In October, 2014 I meant with the current president of SABE, Tia Nelis, in her office at the University of Illinois in Chicago. I asked her how SABE had addressed it.

"People are so thankful for any support that they fear independence will result on support people being angry and not coming back," she said. "Everyone is afraid at first. Like kicking out non-disabled people from meetings. Our first step is to teach people that it is okay to disagree. Those who believe in us will come back." (Interview, 10/17/14.)

But how to get marginalized people to believe in a new dream? Nancy Ward remembers her first experience with self-advocacy and how its success buoyed her own confidence.

"There was a TV commercial about Special Olympics and they were parading kids with disabilities across a stage. I felt that the worst thing you can do for people with disabilities is to feel sorry for them. If you don't give them the opportunity to grow up you are going to see them as little kids all of their lives." (Dydwab/Bersani, pg.217.)

Using confidence gained from her first exposure to Advocacy First of Lincoln she wrote a letter to the Kennedy Foundation and President Carter. The commercial was removed.

"My self-advocacy skills are real important to me," Ward said. "They taught me how to deal with my feelings about having a disability, the anger and hurt and being made fun of. I learned how to gain confidence in myself. I was able to get more active as a leader, because by then

I had confidence in myself to do that." (Dydwab/Bersani. Pg. 219).

Success breeds confidence. Building on local successes self-advocates met in 1991. Tia Nelis remembers "we all knew that self-esteem comes first in self-advocacy. By 1991 we all knew that we needed a national organization to represent us. That organization is Self-Advocates Becoming Empowered." (Interview, 10/17/14).

A group of people with intellectual and developmental disabilities coming together to form their own national organization was without precedent. Nancy Ward remembers "It's been drummed into our heads for our whole lives that you can't be anything until you have money. With People First of Nebraska we did it before we had money. I tried to explain that we can decide first and look for the money later." (Dydwab/Bersani, pg.220)

"Even though some of the advisors thought we were having 'pie in the sky'," Ward remembers, "and that we weren't going to be able to do it. That was all the more reason for me to want to do it. It's real difficult when people tell you that you can't do something that you believe in. That just makes you want to do it all the more. But I knew it was possible because I had experience it." Dydwab/Bersani. Pg. 220).

In spite of skepticism from professionals Self Advocates as Leaders was born and as a first order of business adopted a mission statement that includes this phrase "...our organization is run by a board of self-advocates..." The world of disability advocacy had just become real and would never again be the same. Since its founding SABE has indeed 'found the money.' Not rich by any means the organization now gets grants from federal agencies, states, private organizations, DD Councils, etc. The political work, success and sophistication of their skills has been the wonder of the disability world.

But what about the term self-advocate itself? What does it mean? Why was it adopted?

Bernard Carabello, the hero of Willowbrook closure, once told me that he regarded it as 'just another label.' I asked Tia Nelis her thoughts on self-advocate. Is it just another label or an earned badge of honor?

"I don't care what people call it," she answered. "Without it we get lost in the shuffle. Unless we are able, and we have been, to get organizations and government bodies to write in their agendas and rules that we must be at the table we won't be. Supports are expensive and without them our mere presence is meaningless. It is our advocacy that has assured us a voice in the national dialogue."

"When I turned 18 people told me a sheltered workshop was all I could expect. They told me to stay home. I was determined not to allow social isolation to ruin my life. And SABE has put me in a position to try to make sure it does not ruin the lives of others."

Katie Keiling Arnold, an instructor at the Institute of Disability and Human Development at the University of Illinois at Chicago is a trusted non-disabled ally of the movement and works closely with SABE leadership. "When I hear Tia say something like 'try to make sure it does not ruin the lives of others' it makes me appreciate that whatever else one may say about labels they do help to mobilize people. The use of the term self-advocate is important in giving people the opportunity to claim membership in a group." (Interview, 5/12/15).

"Self-advocate has become the preferred term for people with intellectual and developmental disabilities. A lot of people (not part of the movement) use it as a synonym for the whole community. But it is not a descriptor of the whole community. Rather just a number of committed leaders who have earned it," Arnold continued.

I asked her about national priorities for self-advocacy. "Family members have a hard time letting go," she said. "What is needed is more peer support and role models. When I hear Nancy Ward's powerful story I see the need to create more opportunities for people to be in the lead and everyone else get out of the way."

"There are enormous trust issues on both sides. Do professionals and family members really believe self-advocates can do all of this on their own? People with disabilities don't trust professionals. All of them have been told at one time or another that speaking up is inappropriate. It is that professional paternalism that they hate and that must change."

Having created a national organization that actually represents people with disabilities themselves is nothing short of a miracle. To have it become such a success has been a pleasant surprise even for the founders. "I feel we have accomplished a lot,' says Nancy Ward. "Not only in the work we do but in the relationships we have with each other. We all believe in our organization now. We are alive and growing!" (Dydwab/Bersani. Pg. 233.)

The SABE goals were adopted in 1994. Since then all of them have been reached or are at the top of the agenda for change. An ambitious list for any organization.

- Make self-advocacy available in every state including institutions, high schools, rural areas, people living with families, with local support and advisors to help.
- Work with the criminal justice system and people with disabilities about their rights within the criminal justice system.

- Close institutions for people with developmental disabilities labels nationwide and building community supports. (Dydwab/Bersani. Pg. 234.)

Today SABE has become increasingly visible within the national disability rights movement. Steering committee members are frequently invited to sit on national organizations' boards of directors, to attend national meetings, and to speak for themselves at major national conferences. Invited to join in on grant proposals SABE has become so sophisticated that before answering they require the asking organization to put in writing their own national goals and priorities and explain how they correspond to their own goals. More than two decades after its beginning, through federal budget cuts, vicious attacks on disability rights and millions having their services diminished or eliminated, SABE has continued to stay together and continue to develop in strength and influence.

In a country formed with no regard whatsoever for its disabled citizens the mere existence and power of SABE is nothing short of revolutionary. Add to that the paternalism, exclusion, eugenics, incarceration and planned poverty the community has been subjected to and the rise of self-advocacy can be seen for what it is. The one absolutely essential voice and required to break the chains that have held Americans with intellectual and developmental disabilities hostage too long. Nothing about us without us is more than a slogan. Increasingly it is becoming the fact in national policy making. And for that we can thank self-advocates themselves for breaking barriers the professional community never approached.

Twenty five years ago the Americans with Disabilities Act was passed. Since then it has revolutionized much of how the United States thinks of and treats its disabled citizens. At the same time it introduced a whole new chapter in advocacy. Shortly after passage some of these new challenges were wonderfully examined by Marta Russell in her classic book *Beyond Ramps: Disability at the End of the Social Contract.* (Common Courage Press, 1996). But even Russell's critique was one of a person who came of age before the ADA.

Today the so-called "ADA generation" of young advocates who came of age after passage is taking center stage and assuming leadership of the movement. Their viewpoint is quite different. These are people who were guaranteed a free and appropriate public education in the least restrictive environment. Spared institutionalization they look back on our past with a mix of fury and determination. Appropriately they question assumptions that older advocates simply could not make.

Stephanie Woodward, Director of Advocacy at the Center for Disability Rights in Rochester, New York recently provided me with an example of a freedom of thought characteristic of a new generation of leaders. It there has been a reverential mantra in recent years it has been obeisance to People First Language. ("I am a person with a disability." Not "I am a disabled person.") Progressive as that may have been the ADA generation is not bound by it. "I call myself a disabled person," Woodward told me.

"I am proud of who I am and I want nothing between me and my pride in being a disabled person."

Likewise Ari Ne'eman in founding the Autistic Self Advocacy Network set a wholly new tone. First was the proud adoption of Autistic as the preferred descriptor of what under people first language would be person with autism. Like Woodward he adopted his own 'disability' with pride. By using self-advocacy he telegraphed a solidarity with other oppressed groups. For too long groups fled from fear that they would be confused with people with intellectual disabilities. Happily disability solidarity and a recognition that we are all in this together is the bedrock of new leadership. Also worth noting their lack of need for permission from the establishment to claim their own labels. Breaking with the past their self-adopted labels are ones of pride.

I am optimistic about the future of the disability rights movement. My optimism is not just a Pollyannaish pipe dream. It is rooted in the certain knowledge that now, at last, the voices that matter are disabled voices. Twenty years ago Paul Longmore asked us to consider disabled interests and non-disabled interest. Today the dialogue in dominated by strong voices of disabled interests. Our new leadership is not just young. It is sophisticated, visionary and mostly egalitarian. Yes, rivalry and petty jealousy remains but at the core we now recognize that the movement is bigger than any individual and that cross disability coalitions are the only way forward. To paraphrase President Kennedy this is a generation hardened by war and tempered by a cruel and bitter peace. Onto their shoulders now passes the spirit of Justin Dart, Jr. and all of the millions who came before.

Before concluding I am reminded of Bob Marley who wrote 'Good friends we have had, oh good friends we've lost along the way. In this bright future you can't forget your past. So dry your tears I say."

Who were they? These lost generations of Americans with intellectual and developmental disabilities? The ones of us who lived, died and vanished leaving scarcely a trace. What do we really know of them?

For one thing their numbers are enormous. The Center for Disease Control (CDC) defines developmental disability as a 'group of conditions due to an impairment in physical, learning, language or behavior which begins in childhood and impacts day to day functioning throughout a person's life span." (CDC website. Retrieved 10/29/15).

CDC also believes that these conditions apply to up to 15% of the population.

In 1790 the population of the soon to be born United States of America was 3,900,000.

Applying the CDC criteria that means that as many as 585,000 people with developmental and intellectual disabilities were alive at the time of the constitutional convention. There is no evidence that their lives or existence warranted so much as a footnote.

Today the population of the US is 326,000,000. Accordingly there should be about 4,890,000 people with IDD.

But what about the numbers between then and now? There were millions. That we know. What else do we know?

We know that more than 90% of them lived and died without any access to an education. Not a day inside a school room. No peers to know or to love. For those who lived more than a few years we know of lives of isolation, sleeping in attics, basements, out buildings on the farm. Hidden away. Forgotten.

We know that employment in anything other than home chores or some physical an uncompensated labor was all they could expect. Experts told them so. And experts provided the face saving cover for the generations who happily discounted their very existence.

What we don't know is how many died in infancy of neglect, indifference and lack of medical care. We don't know who many survived in institutions never to feel the hand of a mother's love or the warmth of a family. We don't know how many died needlessly of asphyxia pneumonia acquired from gobbling oatmeal off a wooden spoon ladled out trough like at institutional 'feedings?' Their deaths not related to their disability. Only to the ignorance of the times they were born into.

What made them happy? What frightened them? What were their dreams? What did they hope for? What did they long for? Of that all we can know is that the answers are the same as they are for each of us. They were after all, these lost generations, human beings just like all other human beings. They came into the world. They experienced what they experienced. And they died. Left us without leaving behind any real record of who they were and how they felt.

About them virtually nothing remains. Millions were simply buried in unmarked institutional graves and forgotten. Buried not by name but by the 'inmate' number assigned to them. All vestige of human respect stripped from them due to trait deemed undesirable by the times they were born into.

And that great silence is also the great crime. Let us resolve never to forget them and to honor their memory every day. Amber Smock, Director of Advocacy and External Affairs at Access Living in Chicago challenged us all when she wrote "we are all answerable for the empowerment of others.' Let that empowerment be the living memorial for our lost generations.

Stories referenced in the post script are illustrative. Homely and simple as some may be they capture a snippet in time of the real life of a real person. In them we see all the cacophony of the human experience. Their stories need no interpretation. They need no experts to tell us what they 'really' mean. And in those stories lies our real power and our answer to the eugenics, institutions, poverty, isolation and whatever other horror traveled with us. We get the last laugh. We were always here. We were always people first.

In his dying declaration Justin Dart, Jr. challenged us to participate in a 'revolution of empowerment." To his words let me add those of Paul Longmore.

"The truth is that the obstacles we must overcome are pervasive social prejudice, systematic segregation and institutionalized discrimination. Government social-service policies, in particular, have forced millions of us to the margins of society. These policies have made the American dream inaccessible to disabled citizens.

In saying these things I risk getting myself labeled as a maladjusted disabled person, a succumber to self-pity, a whining bitter cripple who blames non-disabled people for his own failure to cope with his condition. That charge—or the fear that we might provoke it—has intimidated many of us into silence."

As I said, some of us are going to have to risk telling the truth." (Longmore, Pg. 98)

Remembering Tracy Latimer, Ethan Saylor, Sandra Jenson, Ashley X and the forgotten millions.

"I am with you always. Lead On!
Justin Dart, Jr.

POSTSCRIPT

Moments in Time
Americans with Developmental/Intellectual Disabilities in their own words

"Feelings of fear and of being struck down are at the door of my soul. The only place I can be set free is out of society. I run to the mountains. Leaving everything behind me I run full speed into the open field. The ground beneath is solid and secure."
People First Connection, #44.

As noted in the introduction a number of first person accounts of the disability experience have been omitted due to some legal issues. Specifically the impossibility of obtaining commercial transaction releases from the authors. Many of whom are widely scattered or deceased.

As a representation of those stories I have included two. Both were done by my daughter Eleanor who is available and happily signed a release. I have no issue with the release question. At the same time the stories are important. If you desire a non-commercial copy of them kindly send me an email and I will post them to you. Address is mtbclarion@gmail.com.

HOW TO TREAT PEOPLE WITH DISABILITIES

Eleanor S. Bailey

I have a disability and I have a lot of friends who have disabilities. Here are my suggestions on how I want people to treat me.

Treat me with respect.

Understand that I need to make my own choices.

Do not help me all the time because it feels like I am not learning anything.

If I need help I can ask for it.

Do not boss me around and tell me what to do.

Treat me like a friend.

Do not call me names.

Respect that there are some physical things I cannot do. I have a fragile neck.

Say nice things about me and the things I do—compliments.

If I tell you I don't understand please repeat it. But please do not get annoyed with me. I am doing my best.

Language: A person who has a disability is a person just like any other person. When you talk about a person with a disability do not say their disability first. So, say, 'the person who is deaf' instead of 'the deaf person.' Some words about people with disabilities are mean. Do not use words like dumb, retarded, crazy, deformed, lame or defective.

With a person who is blind: Let the person know you are there and who you are. If they have a guide dog do not play with the guide dog. You can offer help but do not help unless the person wants help.

<u>With a person who is deaf:</u> To get the attention of a person who is deaf gently tap them on the shoulder.

<u>With a person in a wheelchair:</u> Do not touch the wheelchair without permission. Do not push the wheelchair unless you have offered to help first and the person said that they want your help.

<u>With a person who has trouble talking:</u> If you do not understand what the person is saying ask them to repeat it. Do not pretend you understand when you do not.

You should treat people with disabilities like you would anyone else. If you are not sure if something is okay you should ask the person with the disability. It is always okay to ask questions.

FINDING MY LABEL

Eleanor S. Bailey

This year some little girls came to my school. I heard some people say "they have Down syndrome." On Saturday I asked my mom "do I have Down syndrome?" Mom said that I do.

I went to my bedroom and closed the door. I didn't cry but I shut my door and was mad and upset. I didn't want to have Down syndrome.

On Monday I went to school. I told my teacher, Mrs. Karr, that I had an announcement to make. She gave me the microphone and I said "I have two things to say. First I have Down syndrome and second I am really afraid that none of you will like me anymore."

My friends were really nice. They said that they already knew that and that they still liked me. Some of them cried. I got lots of hugs.

But I am still not happy. On Wednesday my dad and I got on an airplane and flew to Chicago. On the airplane I listened to my Walkman. I have a song that goes 'clang, bang, rattle, bing, band I make my noise all day.' I thought that is what I can do. Even with Down syndrome I can still make my noise.

We went to the TASH Annual meeting. There were lots of really cool people there. We stayed in a big hotel. In our room there were two bathrooms. One had a shower and one had a tub. I made a big sign that said "girls" and put it on the door of the one with the tub. I didn't want my dad to come in.

I took lots of baths. I thought that if I took enough baths I could wash my Down syndrome away. I also thought that I would put hair spray on it but my mom and dad won't let me have hair spray. I tried to put sunscreen on it then I wouldn't have to have it all of the time. But my dad said that none of that would work.

I have friends who were at TASH. My really special friend is Tia Nelis. She lives in Illinois. Tia has a disability but when she talks people listen. People really listen. Tia is a leader and she really likes me. I told Tia that I have Down syndrome. I was surprised when she said that she had always known that. She said she didn't care. She said that I am an important person and that Down syndrome is not as important as being a wonderful person. When I grow up I wish I could be Tia.

I have other friends at TASH who told me the same thing. I met a really nice person named Katie. Katie goes to college. Katie has Down syndrome. I talked to my other friend Liz Obermeyer (now Weintraub). Liz has a job and is moving to Maryland which is a state. Liz has a disability but she is a leader too. She is on the board of TASH. Liz goes to lots of meetings and people listen to her too.

I got my name from Eleanor Roosevelt. Lots of bad things happened in her life. I have books about her. She was a leader too. I also know about Rosa Parks, Martin Luther King, Jr, Nelson Mandela and Robert Kennedy. Lots of bad things happened to them but they were strong and were leaders too. My dad says they made people proud of who they are and made them free.

I wish I didn't have Down syndrome. But I do and I am a person with a lot of plans. When I wonder what to do I remember my song. I will do what it says. I will go 'bang, clang, rattle, bing, bang and make my noise all day.' Even though I am sad I know that I can be as tough as anyone. That is what I want to do. Just be me.

Eleanor Bailey